C0-APQ-382

Cincinnati
And Other Plays

MONOLOGUES FOR THE THEATRE

by Don Nigro

SAMUEL FRENCH, INC.

45 WEST 25TH STREET   NEW YORK 10010
7623 SUNSET BOULEVARD   HOLLYWOOD 90046
LONDON   *TORONTO*

Copyright © 1989 by Don Nigro

ALL RIGHTS RESERVED

CAUTION: Professionals and amateurs are hereby warned that plays in CINCINNATI AND OTHER PLAYS is subject to a royalty. It is fully protected under the copyright laws of the United States of America, the British Commonwealth, including Canada, and all other countries of the Copyright Union. All rights, including professional, amateur, motion picture, recitation, lecturing, public reading, radio broadcasting, television and the rights of translation into foreign languages are strictly reserved. In its present form the play is dedicated to the reading public only.

The amateur live stage performance rights to plays in CINCINNATI AND OTHER PLAYS are controlled exclusively by Samuel French, Inc., and royalty arrangements and licenses must be secured well in advance of presentation. PLEASE NOTE that amateur royalty fees are set upon application in accordance with your producing circumstances. When applying for a royalty quotation and license please give us the number of performances intended, dates of production, your seating capacity and admission fee. Royalties are payable one week before the opening performance of the play to Samuel French, Inc., at 45 W. 25th Street, New York, NY 10010; or at 7623 Sunset Blvd., Hollywood, CA 90046, or to Samuel French(Canada), Ltd., 100 Lombard Street, Lower Level, Toronto, Ontario, Canada M5C 1M3.

Royalty of the required amount must be paid whether the play is presented for charity or gain and whether or not admission is charged.

Stock royalty quoted upon application to Samuel French, Inc.

For all other rights than those stipulated above, apply to Samuel French, Inc.

Particular emphasis is laid on the question of amateur or professional readings, permission and terms for which must be secured in writing from Samuel French, Inc.

Copying from this book in whole or in part is strictly forbidden by law, and the right of performance is not transferable.

Whenever the play is produced the following notice must appear on all programs, printing and advertising for the play: "Produced by special arrangement with Samuel French, Inc."

Due authorship credit must be given on all programs, printing and advertising for the play.

ISBN 0 573 62105 5   Printed in U.S.A.   #5773

BILLING AND CREDIT REQUIREMENTS

All producers of any play in this volume *must* give credit to the Author in all programs and in all instances in which the title of the Play appears for purposes of advertising, publicizing or otherwise exploiting the Play and/or production. The author's name *must* appear on a separate line in which no other name appears, immediately following the title of the play, and *must* appear in size of type not less than fifty percent the size of title type.

No part of this book may be reproduced, stored in a retrieval system, or transmitted in any form, by any means, including mechanical, electronic, photocopying, recording, or otherwise, without the prior written permission of the publisher.

Anyone presenting the play shall not commit or authorize any act or omission by which the copyright of the play or the right to copyright same may be impaired.

No changes shall be made in the play for the purpose of your production unless authorized in writing.

The publication of this play does not imply that it is necessarily available for performance by amateurs or professionals. Amateurs and professionals considering a production are strongly advised in their own interests to apply to Samuel French, Inc., for consent before starting rehearsals, advertising, or booking a theatre or hall.

3

CINCINNATI

The set is a lectern on a bare stage.

Cincinnati began as a video project shot in the fall of 1977 in Iowa City, Iowa, and featured Sue Hickerson, with Carl Apollo, Jo Vetter, Ayers Baxter and others, under the supervision of Franklin Miller. It was edited by Mary Locke, who also did most of the camera work.

The present stage version was first produced at Indiana State University in Terre Haute, Indiana in April of 1981, and again there in April of 1982, both productions featuring Janice Dukes as Susan, with lighting design by Joseph Chile, and directed by Gary Stewart.

The play was also presented in staged reading at the Yale School of Drama in May of 1982, featuring Lynn Siefert as Susan and directed by the playwright, and in a workshop format in the fall of 1986 at Ensemble Studio Theatre in New York, with Lynn Goodwin.

There is one character, Susan, a young woman of 30.

Cincinnati

(*A moment. The play begins with general lighting and only very gradually does the light begin to focus more and more on the speaker, until! by the end she will be in a glaring spotlight with only darkness around her. After a moment SUSAN Enters. She is thirty, attractive, intelligent, thin and nervous, with some strain showing as she Enters. She is perhaps a bit out of breath at first. She carries books and a manila folder from which she takes notes on yellow paper which she arranges on the lectern. She seems to be using this action to give herself time to compose herself. Finally she looks out, seeming still bewildered or pre-occupied, clears her throat twice, and begins to speak.*)

SUSAN. Today I think it's time we talked about — (*She stops, looking around, irritated, as if at a noisy class.*) Today I think finally we should talk about the illusion — (*She stops again, clearly distressed.*) Today we'll talk — please be quiet — about — (*pause*) — about other people. (*gaining some force and confidence*) Today we're going to talk about other people. A subject which I am certain will fascinate you as much as it does me. (*She is attempting to light a cigarette.*) And intimately related, of course, to the problem of other people, of course — (*She can't seem to get the cigarette lit.*) — fire has a mind of its own, doesn't it? (*She tries again.*) The problem of other people is — (*She gives up.*) — intimately related — I've failed, you see — is intimately related — to light my cigarette — to the problem — no doubt I've failed at much else, too, of course, but in this case I confine refer-

5

ence to the lighting of one cigarette — is intimately related, as I said, to the whole issue of pain.

One may wonder, like the sensitive executioner, if one's own pain can be shared by other people in any recognizable way. Is there such a thing as other people's pain? The pain of those one loves or has loved. The pain of those one wishes to feel pain. One's own pain as understood, if at all, by others. Can one be certain of anything in such matters? (*She tries again to light the cigarette.*) Uncertainty seems to be the rule rather than the exception in this and most other matters, don't you think? As it is, of course, in modern physics, which has something in common, when you think about it — (*She gets the match lit.*) — a miracle — (*She is watching the flame.*) — with the Heraclitian doctrine that fire is the basis of all things. (*She seems hypnotized by the flame.*) If we presume that by fire Heraclitus meant — (*The flame burns her fingers. She waves it out.*) — ouch. Pain, you see. If we presume he meant something like energy, what we call energy now, we can repeat what Heraclitus says almost word for word, we can accept his assertion that all things are made of fire, that things begin in fire and end in fire, that energy is fire and fire is the cause for all change in the world, hence all pain.

There is either change, of course, or there is death. The absence of change is death, although the presence of change is not necessarily life, I suppose, but in any case where life is concerned change is more or less synonymous with or at least always accompanied by a certain amount of suffering. So there is either death or suffering. Which brings us back to what suffers, that is, to other people, and to the self, let us say. We can take, if you like, or even if you don't like, for it's MY class, isn't it, yes, it's comforting to believe so, anyway, but take, for example, any trivial encounter, suppose a woman, say, a woman goes into another woman's office, on any given autumn day.

There are typewriters clicking away like teeth, and people moving back and forth like hot little robots, and in the office a very strange art object on a cabinet, a machine with false teeth that click when a small lever is pulled. And suppose the woman whose office it is, asks the woman whose office it isn't, how she is, is she all right, is everything hunky dory, is life just ducky, is it a bowl of unbitten cherries, how, in short, how IS she?

Now does this woman really CARE? Does the woman whose office it is really accept that the woman whose office it is not has any recognizable feelings in the first place? And if she did accept this, would it in fact be necessarily true? And if it were in fact true, would the woman whose office it is give a good flying fuck at the moon anyway? If the woman whose office it isn't was worth bus fare to the bathroom anyway it would be HER office, wouldn't it, and NOT the office of the woman whose office it is, the woman with the clicking teeth, hereafter referred to as the office woman.

I understand you've been having a rough time of it, says office woman, and the teeth machine behind her pauses to take a breath.

Rough time? asks the woman who is not the office woman, the woman from Cincinnati, let's call her a lecturer, say, a lecturer in philosophy, or in literature, or in the philosophy of literature, which is a wonderful subject because those who teach it may be thoroughly incompetent in both subjects at once, or in the literature of— well, she is from Cincinnati, say, and this is not her office, and she knows it, let's call her Susan, it's a nice name, my parents liked it, it's even MY name, is this then autobiography, you ask, or thinly veiled autobiography, perhaps, or is it auto body repair, or auto-eroticism, or is it — (*Pause. She seems to wake up and realize that she has lost control of her lecture. She swallows once, pulls her hair back from her face nervously, and smiles.*) Excuse me. I'm babbling, aren't I? Of course I am. Do you think I'm beautiful? If I were to play with my shirt off, would you like that, could we make Iliads? (*Pause. She looks out at them.*) But I digress. (*pause*)

So the woman whose office it is not, who is from Cincinnati and whose name may or may not be Susan, asks, innocently, eyes wide, Rough time? What rough time? She hasn't been to Cincinnati for some time, so perhaps she has not in fact been conscious of having a rough time, although at some time in the past of course she may indeed have had a very rough time, possibly in Cincinnati, say. Does the plot coagulate a bit? No? Sorry.

I'm fine, says Susan.

You're feeling better then, says office woman smoothly, very carefully, for she is a chairlady, as opposed to a chairman, or a chairperson, or a charlady, and she does everything ever so carefully, doesn't she? And Cincinnati Susan sees that when the office woman smiles her teeth are like the teeth of the machine behind her on the shelf, and in the outer offices the typewriters are clicking away like a room full of false teeth.

Better than what? asks Susan, with perhaps just the slightest trace of malice in her voice.

Oh, says office woman, too much to do, not enough time.

I have plenty of time, says the victim Susan, lying through her teeth.

Take a rest, if you'd like, says Mrs Office. We could take over your classes now and again, sometimes.

Just sometimes? asks Susan. Why just sometimes?

Mrs Office smiles back at her like a dead fish.

Has someone complained? I ask.

You know students, she says. They expect us to be perfect. They allow us no mistakes. They think they're the center of the universe, don't they?

Not MY universe, I reply.

It's all right to take a rest, she says. You needn't be ashamed if you need a rest.

I rest. The teeth click. Did someone complain, then? One of my students? Which one? I want names and dates. Serial numbers. Unusual body markings. Sexual histories.

We know you've had a tragedy, she says, but we all have tragedies. I think sometimes, she begins wisely, a fount of wisdom, I want to jam the letter opener up her nostril by this point, anticipating the great wisdom she is about to puke up onto my shoes—

Sometimes I think, she says—

Congratulations, I want to say, I never would have guessed it, but I don't say this, of course, I listen politely, face all bright and shiney, breasts fallen just a bit, for I am now thirty, you know, and the breasts begin, just a bit, just a bit to fall, to have fallen, before this, even, but—

Sometimes I think, she goes on, this a particularly long thought for her, I think sometimes we're being tested by God, to see how well we can handle things. It's a test of character.

I imagine God handing out number two pencils and telling us to be sure and put our names on the test.

You mustn't let this defeat you, she concludes. I can smell fresh earth, freshly mown grass, woods.

I'm a good teacher, I say.

I'm sure you are, says Mrs Office and her magic teeth.

You know the material. If your performance is
sometimes —
    What?
    Sometimes — she searches for the right word.
    Sometimes what?
    Oh, well, perhaps, just a shade, I don't know, erratic.
    I begged her pardon promptly. This usually works. She
retreated like a sick hyena.
    Oh, she says, looking at her watch with the subtlety of a
rhinoceros, it's after five, we've got to go, don't we, don't
want to be late for the big orgy, do we? You take care of
yourself, she says. Things have a way of falling into place.
And she ushers me out of the office like a mother putting
her child to bed. And then, as I am leaving, she has the
nerve to ask me if I have a light. Do I have a light? Am I a
lighthouse?
    Can you see what I'm driving at? Given this very in-
structive example can you honestly defend the idea that
other people have any right to exist? Why not just kill
them all and be done with it? Because because because
because because. The pain, you see, it drives us together
like goats.
    We learn what pain is from our own case. I can't be
sure exactly what you're talking about when you refer to
your own pain. You may mean something very different
than I do. Pain is, for the solipsist, a private object. There
is no sharing of pain. There is no sharing. There is nothing to share with. And no one has any business telling me
whether or not I'm using the word 'pain' in the proper
sense. The proper sense is MY sense. Isn't it? Who else
can understand what I mean by such a word? You? You
may not even *feel* pain, for all I know. Perhaps the child
dying in the fire feels nothing. As far as I can ever know, I
may be the only conscious being in existence. The world,
in short, is MY world.

Oh, one divides the world, true, but not so much into things as into webs of connections. It's always the same spiderweb. Dirt crumbles from the same hands into the same grave. The same collections of forces acting between particles of self, the world appearing as a complicated tissue of events in which connections of different kinds alternate and overlap and combine and perform sexual acts in a variety of unnatural positions to determine the texture of the whole animal which is the god which is the fire which is the death always ultimately of the soft beloved fragile created thing or other self I make and am and kill.

So, suppose this woman Susan who is more or less desperate for reasons which are not entirely clear perhaps goes into yet another office, and there is the sound of a young girl laughing which sounds like a child's laughter but is in reality the laughter of a student, a soft blond girl who is standing close to a young professor by a desk, so close they may be touching, her face flushed, and as Susan walks into the room the girl turns away quickly from the young professor and Susan can see clearly the erect nipples of the girl's young breasts through her shirt. This woman Susan thinks of her own sad brooding nipples, covered in sweaters and sad, lips that sucked them once, tiny mouth, little fingers, there in a bundle, I was this once, she thinks, and my daughter would be this once, too, might have, the life sucked out of the breasts, we use them to draw men and feed children, are marked by them, trapped, lost. Mystery of mammal life. Vulgar, grotesque and vulgar, like all organic business. The tiny mouth of the baby girl-child nipple mouth and little fingers working. It hurts. Pain, you see.

Excuse me, says Susan.

No, says the young professor, we were just having a private conference.

I'll come back later, says Susan.

No, she's going, says the young professor. And to the girl with the breasts he says to do those exercises they talked about and then come back and see him, all right?

The student leaves, blushing a bit and goes past Susan in the doorway, breasts almost touch, mouth of little girl on breasts, the charred black flesh, the smell. A dissertation on roast child. Stop it.

Playground noises, not from here, no, this is the university, sex is what we play here, but in her head, children screaming happily, impaled on stakes perhaps, then not so happy, soft.

Office door closing. Closing doors.

Nice girl, says the young professor, a boy wonder, he, whiz kid, Mr Wizard, Young Doctor Malone. She needs a lot of help, though. Surprising how many of them do.

I'm sure they do, says Susan.

So Mr Wizard asks me how I am, and I say I'm fine, and here's your book, I say. He says we really should see more of each other. I for one would like to see more of him. I'd like, for a start, to see what he keeps in his pants. A gun, perhaps? Is that a banana in your pocket, Doctor Kildare, or have you hidden the rectal thermometer I keep for my horse?

You're so quiet, he tells me. What do you do with yourself?

I masturbate, of course, but I don't tell him this. Probably he knows. I tell him I read a lot, take walks.

She's a botany major, he says.

Who is? I ask, all innocence and wide eyes, never suspecting that his mind is still lost in the land of Miss Baby Tits, the nippled wonder. That any girl should be nineteen I find obscene. I rhymed.

That girl, he says. I'm trying to convert her to the humanities.

I'll just bet you are, I think. Then he tells me how much he admires me. I can't imagine why, but I like this. He says I am so self-contained, I seem so self-contained, yes, I think, like a hermetically sealed bucket of vomit, but I don't say this, I just smile modestly at him. Then he asks me how I am in that peculiar tone of voice one uses to address the senile, the infant, the mentally deficient, the insane.

I ask him if he thinks I look like I've been having a rough time. He says he hadn't noticed. Am I?

I'm fine, I say. How are you? I am fine. A letter from camp. How are you? I'm fine. The dog is fine. The cat is fine.

Don't you get lonely in that apartment all by yourself? he asks. I'd think you'd be afraid to live alone like that.

You live alone, I point out.

That's different, he says.

How is it different? I ask.

I'm a man, he says.

This of course explains everything. I want at this point to hang this man up in stirrups and jam my fountain pen into his private parts, all the while talking about the weather, but I let him patronize me, don't make waves, what's the point, they already think you're insane.

I think I'd be afraid NOT to live alone, I say.

Come and see me some time, he says. You'll go nuts like that.

I dislike this expression. Or blind, I think. I'll go blind.

I meet a lot of those, he says.

This man has a PhD and an IQ of about six and a half, and he looks like a deodorant commercial, but he survives, some handsome cunning, and I bow to his stupid charm, he is my version of the nippled wonder-piglet, I too am weak flesh, we are attracted by the most idiotic creatures, he meets a lot of those. Telephone ringing. Is it for me? Is the letter for me? It never is. Hope and dread. Good news, bad news. Go mad, spend all your time scratching the cat and singing Christmas carols, watch the fire. Elements. Dissertation on roast. Stop it.

We have known of course for some time that the universe is basically cannibalistic in nature, that each part survives by devouring the others, that consciousness feeds upon consciousness like vermin upon cattle or maggots on dead children. We are all dying flesh, our moments are stolen, our loves idiotic, our values pathetic, life is a small flame in a very dark room and we consume ourselves, born dying. How then can one possibly be expected to conduct oneself with dignity under such circumstances? Marcus Aurelius grows mute and foolish compared to the horror on the porch swing, the nightmare in the rubble, the lurker in the shithouse.

One is surrounded by others who judge one's performance at each moment and at each moment find us wanting. Our situation is precarious, we are guilty, we are at the mercy of any drooling moron who wishes to point this out to us. His own guilt or stupidity or malice does not erase our own. Nothing does, we are bloody up to our elbows, we carry the guilt within us, guilty by definition, devourers of carnage, stealers of life, and no amount of scientific obfuscation or religious rigamarole or humanistic slobber can eliminate the simple and undeniable reality of our original sin.

But if I can never know other people's pain, I can never know if they are real, for we are made real by suffering, and so I can never really attribute guilt to other people. But there is guilt, I can smell it, and so it follows inexorably then that all the guilt is MINE. Because I have perceived that to be is to suffer, and I cannot presume that others ARE, and the amount of pain I sense in the world remains enormous and I am therefore left to swallow it all myself. I am thus the cannibal who eats herself. I am the universe dreaming that it devours itself.

I continue to exist because I suffer. I suffer because I continue to exist. If I could stop suffering, would I disappear? Would everything else? Would I lay rotting on the steps like the witch and the house melt like wax or the child's flesh screaming? Listen to her screaming. Listen.

Footsteps in an empty corridor. Empty house.

Playground noises. I am turning over the pages of a book in the library, colored reproductions of paintings, naked people dying, being stepped on by horses and such, the hell of Hieronymus Bosch, flames in the back of dark buildings, the horrors, naked people chased by carnivorous instruments, impaled on stakes, and the kind man with the sad face bends over my shoulder and looks.

The garden of earthly delights, he says.

I look up. His kind face, sad. I have seen you at the playground. You sit and watch, he says.

Yes, I say. His breath smells of peppermints.

Which of the children is yours?

None of them, I say.

Oh, he says. Pause. You seem to be a very deep thinker, he says. You seem always lost in thought.

Lost in thought. Lost in space. Lost in the jungle. Tarzan and Jane have sex in the treehouse. Lost.

I often watch you, I must confess, he says, kind man with a sad face, sad man with a kind face, sad face with a kind man, peppermint. You seem, he says, always to be paying attention to something the rest of us can't see.

This man is so familiar. It seems as if I've dreamed about him.

Excuse me, he says. I must go take something apart.

And he shuffles away down the corridor with his cane, slight limp, breathing a bit heavily. Such sad kind eyes he has. Where have I seen this man?

At night the telephone rings and when I pick it up I hear Vivaldi, the Four Seasons, the Autumn section. Hello, I say. An idiotic thing to say to Vivaldi, I know, but what is one to do? Hello. The music continues. Then a click. Silence.

Or now she is riding in a car driven by the office woman, who is enjoying herself greatly now through penance. I hope you don't mind, says Mrs Office, my tactless reference to your little girl. It just slipped out.

I told her I was fine. She continued to twist the knife.

My sister's house burnt down last summer, she said. I know how difficult it must be. The dog was killed. It was horrible. They said it was a cigarette.

It wasn't a cigarette, I say, flicking ashes out the window as I speak.

My sister's was, she says.

Mine wasn't, I say.

I thought it was, she says.

It was something else, I say.

Oh, she says. Long pause here. Driving. Does your husband still live in Cincinnati?

Shovel digging dirt. Crows.

I don't know. I'm never going back there. All that is gone. There is no more Cincinnati.

I'm sorry I brought it up, she says. It was such a nice little dog, she says. I cried, she says. You must have felt much worse, she says. Is this where I turn? What shall we have for lunch?

I think of this woman impaled on a stake in a field, naked, being eaten alive by carrion birds.

The catch is caring, you see, and this comes from need.

Need makes caring and caring makes pain, and pain produces the real perception of value, value is something one does not have, will never have, something lost. One is trapped in a world prison where one loses by definition and is forced into a life of intellectual and emotional frenzy. Continuing to live becomes eventually the moral equivalent of suicide.

There are leaves burning, a bonfire in the late afternoon, footsteps in leaves, and birds, mourning doves. I am walking in the woods. A dream. This is a dream. We are such stuff. A man is tending a fire, turned away slightly from me. He looks from the back rather like a goat.

Hello, I say. He looks at the fire. Is this your property? I ask. I suppose it is. I take walks and then I get lost. Exploration and discovery. I discover I'm lost.

He says nothing. I feel I'm dreaming. The smell of the burning and of some animal, perhaps. The fire hypnotizes. A primary element. All things are full of gods. You can't step into the same fire twice. Have I got that wrong? The goatlike man remains turned away from me. It smells all goaty. The gods are released when the leaves are burnt, they escape into the air, you can hear them playing in the leaves, laughing in the woods, the goatgod chases the naked maiden, clublike phallus, red pig eyes, capturing the white flesh, you stand still in the woods and the gods are silent, move and they laugh. Pan the horned god. All the lurking evil of old vegetation. Watching me. Is this where I turn? And what shall we eat? And how do I get back from here? I wake up in my own bed sweating, twisted in the covers. I can't sleep. I get up and take a shower. The water and the nakedness arouse me. I can't sleep. I am desperate. There are faces at the windows, outside looking in.

Symbols. The snow falls and is death, all things are symbols, a personal and ruthless message from dead gods to do this or be that, reminder of one's essential degradation by the world, the snow, the night, faces I have seen in windows, I have seen through the mask of symbols and I know them, know their secrets and this does not comfort me. Each event is a carefully constructed web of symbols that makes the monstrous thing continue to jerk and move. We are all being killed slowly by symbols. We are all being driven mad by this knowledge.

Footsteps down a hollow corridor.

Crickets, night in a university town, she knocks on the young professor's door, a long moment, the door opens.

Idiotic greetings. Prince Valiant is shirtless, barefoot, his fly not done up perfectly, giving the distinct impression that he has quite recently been more or less naked. She apologizes for bothering him.

You're up late, he says.

I know, she says. That I'm late. That I'm up. And it's late.

Is there something wrong? he asks, looking behind him nervously. He looks like a soap opera hero who has forgotten his lines. He has made not the slightest indication that he intends to invite her in.

No, she says, I was just, no.

Oh, he says, and there is a long pause in which she realizes that he is not going to ask her in. But with the blind stupidity of the desperate she decides to ignore this.

I just couldn't sleep, she says.

I'm out of sleeping pills, sorry, he says.

Endless pause.

I'd invite you in, he says, finally, but—

No, that's all right, she says, very anxious not to hear the reason.

I've got a big day tomorrow, he says.

Yes, she says. She doesn't move. They stand there. Cricket sounds.

Did you have a bad dream? he asks.

Sometimes, she says. She sees that another great awful pause is coming, so she vomits out that she used to dream always about empty buildings, deserted streets, places with no people. Except once there was a man at the end of a long dark corridor. I kept walking towards him, my footsteps echoing, from far away the sound of children screaming on a playground, he was the only person I ever saw in my dreams, his face was in the shadows, but I somehow knew that it must be a very kind and infinitely sad face, and as I got closer I became gradually over-whelmed with the terror that he was going to eat me.

Another interminable pause. Young Andy Hardy looks blankly at her.

What do YOU dream about? she asks, idiotically.

Squirrels, he says.

Another pause. Oh, she says. God, is this man stupid.

Well, he says, starting to move back and closing the door a bit as he does so.

Desperate and drowning she blurts out the first thing she can think of to stop him: Do you have some coffee?

I drink tea, he says.

Do you have tea? she asks.

No, he says, I don't. The door closes a little further.

Could I please just use your phone, please, she says, now almost frantic. Something's wrong with mine, I don't know what, I keep getting calls when no one's there, only sometimes I hear music, I don't know what, if I could just make one call—

She sees on his face that he sees now that he is never going to get rid of her unless he lets her use the phone. So he sighs like Camille and with very little pretense of being polite any more he opens the door wide for her to enter, making an ironic welcoming gesture that manages to combine compassion and contempt in rather equal amounts.

And feeling great relief and only a little shame she starts in the door, when at the end of the hall in the living room appears a tall brunette wearing a bath towel, and not very efficiently at that, for she holds it in front between her breasts and it comes open just a bit at the hips, a bit of tummy and hint of a tuft of hair below just for a moment visible, and she is saying, What happened to all the toilet paper?

She sees Susan and stops, covering up some, which is ridiculous when you think about it. Oh, sorry, says the brunette.

It's in the kitchen, says Sunny Jim to me.

The toilet paper? asks the brunette.

The telephone, says the young professor.

What am I supposed to do, call OUT for toilet paper, or what? says the brunette. These two must have wonderfully complex intellectual discussions.

Put some clothes on, why don't you, says Mr Clean.

Susan is backing away and saying thank you and goodnight and goodnight and thank you and he says to the brunette, what do you want to run around like that for, put something on, or I'll give you a C minus, you slut.

And the brunette says, it's all gone. We were full up yesterday. Where did it all go? It's all gone. This question clearly obsesses her as the problem of evil obsessed Kierkegaard. The door closes. This is the function of doors.

Susan walks in the night quickly and blindly and feels her mind beginning to hum as if it is about to snap like a cable.

One wonders if sanity is a democracy, or if truth is? In Plato's cave the shadows were truth. In our world, truth is what others want us to see. With one part of my mind I know perfectly well that this is a trap I am stepping into, that I am systematically humiliating myself over and over again for a series of illusions. I think truth is a conspiracy directed against the insane. We're not allowed truth, the others keep it to themselves. The other people, the god-people, the demons. Imaginary, they are. They torment us. They come at us making their stupid squeaks and telling us what to think about ourselves. They judge, berate, make dirty our moments, laugh at us behind our backs. Other people are a conspiracy of deceitful wicked lies, but only if we are stupid enough to believe in them.

Leaves burning. A bonfire. They light fires on the moor. Emptiness.

The solipsist escapes all this. She believes that only she herself exists and only the places she is at now exist, that other places are disassembled by the evil demons in her dream that seem to pose as other people that in fact do not exist except in her nightmare.

We can picture her imagining she'd caught a glimpse of them around corners, detected a small crack in the landscape of artificial worlds of buildings and geography these creatures had set up for her. Why would these creatures perform such an elaborate masquerade for her? Some infinite malice? And how could she prove it? By doing something totally unexpected, catching them off guard? What would these hideous creatures least expect her to do?

Cups on dishes. A restaurant on the highway. She has gotten into her car and driven. She goes into the restaurant and looks for a place to sit and there, in a corner booth, with gravy-stained plate and part of a piece of pie pushed away, finishing a cup of coffee, is the sad man with the kind face from the playground and the library.

Hello again, he says, noticing her. We seem destined to meet from time to time.

Yes, she says, a bit disoriented, but lonely, and glad, really, to see him.

You're a long way from home, he says. Halfway to Cincinnati.

Yes, I say. I know where I am.

Would you like to join me? he asks.

She would. She does.

What are you doing out here? she asks.

Coming back, he says. From Cincinnati. A convention. Hordes of English teachers, hideous thing. But. What about you? You're a long way from home.

You said that, I point out.

Did I? he says. Sorry. I look at him. I've hurt his feelings.

I was just driving, I say.

To Cincinnati? he asks, drinking his coffee and looking at her with his great sad eyes, a compassionate smile on his face, like a benign middle-aged Christ. Something about him makes me trust him.

I used to live in Cincinnati, I say.

Going back for a visit, then? he says, sipping his coffee.

Well, she says, I don't know, exactly, what I think I'm doing, I guess I just wanted to see it, to convince myself that—I guess that it's still there, that it hasn't been, I don't know, that it hadn't somehow gone away because it was obvious that I would never go back there.

And having said this, actually said it, I begin to feel ridiculous.

Go away? he asks. Where would it go?

I don't know, I don't know, and now I am crying a bit, stupid thing to do.

You're upset, he says.

I lie to him of course. Earth buries, water drowns, air suffocates, fire devours, all the faces of God have teeth and all of them are eating me and killing me and all of them I think ARE me. This is what the solipsist says, does, is. She is the god devouring herself, tormented by projections of herself, God is a fire in her head, burning, she is a dead self that will not stop devouring. In communion we eat God. In the world he eats us. We are the cannibal bread and wine, and all of you are the lies of her teeth, the stench of her breath, you are the rude exhalations of God, you are a deception which does not deceive. Cruel and imaginary, you are nobody and nothing and I speak to you desperate and you are ME. But I FEEL that I am, I FEEL that I am, in a way quite unlike the way I might feel that YOU are, so I'm trapped in my own lie, forced to deal with these murderous imaginary demonic projections of my own depravity.

Cups on china.

You remind me of someone, says the kind-faced man. Do I?

My ex-wife, he says. It's true. She was a lovely woman, very warm, funny, a good person, but she was always figuring in her head, a little desperately. I never knew what about. I suppose she was simply terrified of other people. I don't know. She made up the most incredible fantasies, dinosaurs looking in the windows at night, conspiracies, monsters, I don't know what. She lost her mind, finally.

I'm sorry, I said, feeling a cold damp spot in the center of my brain.

It could happen to any of us, I suppose, he said. None of us is ever all that far from the edge, I think.

And I remind you of her? I asked.

Oh, he said, laughing, very engagingly, not that way,

no, just the — forgive me, I don't know you very well, do I? A few chance encounters at the playground and here I am telling you the story of my life.

But I felt that I knew him. I'd known this man in a dream somewhere. It was just — I could almost remember, just — but then the waitress came, an ancient woman with large yellow eyes like a lizard her throat and boney fingers and it was gone.

I see myself often as a kind of dream I'm having, and I share with the child the illusion of central position and the very natural feeling that she is the center of all things and that all other things, people, animals, geographical locations, exist only when she is directly perceiving them.

(The gradual creeping in of the light has created by this point a circle of light around her of perhaps six feet in diameter. This spot will follow her from this point on and gradually get smaller and move in on her face.)

What happens, then, to geographical locations, say, when the solipsist isn't there? I rather fancy that they are taken apart for future use. These instruments of torture are then reassembled, I imagine, in different combinations elsewhere, like pieces of theatrical scenery. And so the nightmare continues. Continues until when?

Why did you say you were going to Cincinnati? asks the man.

I don't know, I answer, I'm confused now, perhaps I'm not, perhaps I don't need to, it all seems so silly when I sit here and talk to you, I feel like I'm waking up from a bad dream. You've just been there? To Cincinnati?

Yes.

And how is it there? I mean —

Oh, he says, it's the same. Parts of it are very nice. As American cities go, you know, it's very pleasant, very civilized — well, you know that better than I do. I've only been there a few times. It's quite a nice place.

Yes, I say, yes, I remember. And suddenly I want to cry, remembering, I want to cry.

It IS still there, he says, smiling. And on his kind face I see compassion and understanding and I realize that this man is speaking to a madwoman, and I am very ashamed.

Of course it is, I say. Of course it is. How stupid I am. How very, very stupid I am.

Well, he says, have a pleasant trip, and he recommends a hotel there.

No, I say, I think perhaps I should just go home. Yes. I think perhaps I should. I have a class to teach, you know, my students, they're children, really, they're like my children, one can't run out on one's children that way, can one? I hope I'll see you again some time, I say.

At the playground, perhaps, he says.

No, I say. At the library, perhaps. Thank you. Thank you very much. And impulsively I lean over and kiss him on the cheek. He smells of peppermint and something else. I get into the car and I drive back to the university, and here I am.

Here you are, says Mrs Office, smiling, in the morning. I am in the office of Mrs Office, trying to explain all this to her. She understands. She does understand. I've been so unfair to her. To realize, I say, that I belong here, that I have a job here, that this is my life and that it matters and that, that it's REAL, this is like coming back to life, I say. I am Lazarus come back from the dead.

Listening to him talk about his poor wife, I say, for some reason, my own life seemed to fall into place, I realized that I was driving myself insane over something I can't do anything about. I'm here now and I have a new life. And I mustn't waste this. My students are real, and they need me. I mustn't go mad. I must get a hold of myself and live my life. The world has many wonderful things in it, still. I must teach, I must be a good teacher, and above all I must never doubt, I must never doubt.

You're a very brave woman, says the young professor, who is in the office with us. I respect you very much.

We're both very proud of you, says Mrs Office. All of us are.

I look at their kind faces, and I see that I do have friends. They are not perfect, they are not perhaps enormously intelligent or interesting, but they are real persons, they exist and in their own way they mean well, they wish me no harm. It's like waking up from a bad dream and finding that the world makes sense after all.

Then it's time for my class. This class. So I thank them again for being so understanding, and I apologize again for being so difficult, and I rush out, very excited and happy, to teach this class. I am walking happily down the corridor to this classroom, hearing the echo of my footsteps down the corridor, and I realize that in my haste I have left my books and notes in the office of Mrs Office. So I go back to the office to get them and I stop just outside the door I have left not ten seconds ago because I hear voices, three voices, and one very familiar voice is saying—

I think we've got her now.

She seems convinced, says Mrs Office.

The question is, says the young professor, do we want to risk taking it all down now?

It's been sitting there too long, says the familiar voice. We can use the materials.

She'll never go back now, I'm sure of it, says Mrs Office.

I guess I agree, says the young professor.

Well, I think that's probably it, then, says the familiar voice. I'd better go and see about dismantling Cincinnati.

I open the door and the three of them are standing there, the office woman and the young professor and the sad man with the kind face. They look up at me, and in that look, that incredible three-faced look as the heads first turn in surprise to look at me, I see guilt, caught in the act, caught in the act, guilt — this for just a moment but on all three faces, and then immediately the faces are relaxed and friendly again, and oh so very sane and concerned.

What are you doing here? I ask the kind man with the sad face.

Well, he says —

You don't know these people, I say.

He's an old friend of mine, says Mrs Office smoothly. I was just introducing him to Bill. Do you two know each other?

What's all that talk about dismantling? I say.

Dismantling? asks Mrs Office, as if pronouncing a word in a foreign language.

You must have misunderstood, says the young professor.

Do you feel all right? asks the office woman.

I feel FINE, I say. You said you were going to dismantle Cincinnati.

I never said that, says the kind man with the peppermint breath. Your mind is playing tricks again, Susan.

I know you, I say. You're the man in the dream. The goat man. You are.

I look into his face and I see that he feels sorry for me. Something deep inside him feels sorry for me.

Would you like to lie down? asks Mrs Office. And the machine with teeth behind her is laughing at me and grinding its teeth, laughing and grinding.

I turn and run out the door and down the corridor, clutching my books and papers to my breasts, and I stop at the door of my classroom to catch my breath, and I compose myself and I come in the door and I give this lecture. And I know that they are waiting for me back there at the back of the room, in the darkness, waiting. I don't know what they'll do to me now. I would ask you to help me but I know you can't.

You may ask, can I really believe this? Can anybody? I think if you're honest with yourself you can remember a time when you believed this or something like it. You still do. Or you would, if you existed at all. It makes perfectly good sense, it really does, it's the only answer, really.

(The light is now a bright spot on her face, everything else is darkness.)

If one is sure of nothing, one is nowhere. One cannot even doubt, one cannot be sure that one doubts. One is reduced, in the end, to silence. One is reduced to merely looking. One is reduced to pain. Privately. One is a private object. This is perhaps how it should be. For in the end, one's tormentors must also be illusion. If I walk out the door and down the dark corridor, who knows what lurks waiting before me, behind me, at both sides? One discovers, at a certain point in one's life, that the answer is in fact imminently forthcoming. And that is the most

frightening thing of all. (*pause*) Any questions? (*pause*)
Hello? (*pause*) Is anybody there? (*pause*) Empty chairs I
speak to. Empty space. The space between stars. Cold.
And empty. (*pause*) Goodbye, then. (*pause*) You're a
good class. Disappear.

(*A brief moment. Then the light on her face goes out.
Darkness.*)

Nightmare With Clocks

Nightmare With Clocks was first produced in New York in June, 1987 by the Triangle Theatre Company, Michael Ramach and Molly O'Neil. It featured Joel Parkes as Mr Arbuthnot and was directed by Will Cantler.

Nightmare With Clocks

(*An antique store, with many old clocks scattered about.
MR ARBUTHNOT, a man in his forties, goes about
winding clocks as he speaks.*)

MR ARBUTHNOT. I keep having this nightmare, you
see. I have not been prone to nightmares in general,
although it is true I must confess that I have always
tended moderately towards obsession. This is of course
not a very practical way to live, but one does not choose
in such matters, one is chosen, isn't one? I even know, I
think, where this small tendency towards obsession
began. When I was a child, my grandfather, an interesting but rather demented dealer in imports with whom I
lived and who was more or less my only real family,
would appear and disappear from my life with the regu-
larity of a psychopathic cuckoo clock, as his business
took him now to Belgium, now to Switzerland, now to
God knows where, and I was thus thrown much into the
company of a neighbor woman who would look after me
upon such occasions, and whose little girl became, I
think, my first real obsession, an obsession which began,
I believe, if indeed you can say it began anywhere in
particular, one morning when I charged upstairs and
found the neighbor lady giving her daughter a bath. I
stood in the doorway watching this very interesting
procedure — they didn't seem either one of them to
mind, we were, after all, merely children — and I remember that beside me in the hall was an ancient grandfather clock, ticking rather loudly, it seemed to me, and I
remember becoming aware, suddenly, in my simple little complicated five year old brain, that I had stumbled
in unawares upon a secret moment in time, a moment of

33

unspeakable beauty revealed unexpectedly and locked
ever after indelibly in my brain, while all along the real
thing itself was dying as I watched it, in time to the
relentless ticking of the enormous old grandfather clock
beside me. They moved away shortly after that, and I
never saw the little girl again, but the image of her body
in the bath obsessed me forever after, and I do believe my
subsequent childhood and adolescence was a ridiculous
and pathetic series of misplaced and misguided foot-
notes to that experience, that is, one obsession after another with some poor girl or other, and all of them, of
course, ended disastrously, for I remained awkward and
clumsy and not, I must confess, exactly every adolescent
girl's dream, and, more than that, my obsessive nature
frightened them to death, especially as it always seemed
to spring suddenly full blown out at them from nowhere
from a person they had seen heretofore as the gentlest
and most innocuous of souls. The incongruity was too
much for them, it was grotesque, I was grotesque, the
entire matter was, in the end, incredibly grotesque.

Sad. And when such disasters continued into my
young manhood, I decided, finally, that the strain upon
my own psyche and those of the unfortunate young
women I happened to fix my obsession upon was simply
too much to justify continuing, and I began to try and
channel my obsessive nature into something more con-
structive, or at least less embarrassing, and thus I began
to become the man I became, and have been, for some
time, a dealer in antiques, with a special interest in, yes,
clocks. And a very good one, too. And in this way I
managed, over the years, to quiet and divert somewhat
my tendency towards obsession, to get involved, when
absolutely necessary, only with women I knew I could
not possibly become obsessed with, and, in short, to

reach a kind of truce with my neurosis, I found sex with unlovable women and love with antique clocks, and, as compromises go, I thought I had made a rather successful one, that is, until the nightmares began.

They are always more or less the same. I'm in an enormous old house, quite late at night. It's rather dark, and there are many clocks. I hear the ticking as I stand there. I am frightened but exhilarated, as if I am about to do something I should not do, in a place I should not be. There is a great old twisting staircase before me — the floor at the foot of the staircase where I stand is like a giant checkerboard, black and white squares. I look up the twisted staircase and know that what I want is up there, at the top of the steps. I start up the staircase. The steps creak. The ticking of the clocks is louder. In the hall at the top of the stairs sits a large old grandfather clock, its hands nearing two a.m. Beside the clock is a door. I hesitate. I am terrified but I know what I must do. I open the door and look in. There is a bedroom, with a canopy bed, and sleeping there, her hair spread out on the pillow, is the most beautiful young woman I have ever seen. She is very young, eighteen perhaps, her nightgown is white and cut low, and I can see her breasts move up and down gently as she sleeps. I move towards the bed, but as I reach a certain point the grandfather clock in the hallway chimes, once, twice, loud, and I wake up, back in my own bed, sweating and lost, feeling such an enormous sense of having lost a universe of unspeakable value. And for the rest of the night, try as I might, I cannot go back to sleep. And then, a few nights later, the dream recurs. I have just got to thinking it will never happen again, and then one night I find myself in that house again, with those ticking clocks, and I go up the stairs and find the same girl, in the same room, so lovely, and the moment I begin to approach her the grandfather clock in the hall chimes twice and I wake up at home in my bed. The most horrible thing is to hear the first chime and know that when the second one comes everything will have vanished, and I will wake up alone again in my little room behind the antique shop, and only the ticking of the clocks remains. That is my nightmare. Now, of course, I am a reasonably well educated man, and quite capable of psychoanalysing myself about this dream. I can see that the experience with the little neighbor girl, my tendency towards obsession, my lonely life, my profession, the clocks, my sense of getting old with no hope of company, all these things of course and perhaps a bit of ill-digested cheese from time to time have contributed to this particular nightmare, I know this, I understand it, the pieces of it are pieces from my life, it is a creation of the circumstances of my life, but knowing this does not, unfortunately, make it one bit less agonizing. But at least it did seem to provide an explanation. Until the day a certain old gentleman came into my shop. And things — things got somewhat more complex.

This very nice old gentleman came into my shop, a man of some wealth who had fallen onto harder times, who had certain medical expenses which forced him to sell a few items from his collection, and who had heard that I was especially interested in old clocks. He had, he said, at his home, a rather extraordinary collection of antique clocks, and wondered if I might not like to stop by and have a look at one or two of them, it would pain him to part with any of them, of course, but his house had become quite cluttered with them of late, and certain other matters of a personal nature had forced him to think of selling, at least one or two items, would I like to see them? He gave me a card with an address on it, we made a date for a certain afternoon, and, suddenly, the plot had thickened, as it were. The plot had in fact nearly coagulated. You've guessed it already, of course, and you've already decided I'm quite looney. Well, nevertheless.

On a blustery autumn day I made my way to the address the old man had given me, leaves blowing about in the streets, thinking about this and that, and when I came upon the house I thought it looked familiar, it was enormous, and very old, in a once genteel, now decaying part of the city, it was quite beautiful, really, but then, I had visited many old places like this, buying antiques. Of course it would seem familiar. I had spent my life in such places. But when the door opened, and the old man let me into his house, I saw the black and white checkered entry space and looked up the great twisted staircase and I knew, beyond any question, that it was in fact the house in my dream. It was interesting that at this moment I, who had often felt, when dreaming my dream, absolutely convinced of the reality of that house, now, when actually standing inside it and perfectly awake, became convinced I must be dreaming. I felt at that moment a strange mixture of panic and delight wash over me, a kind of excitement which heretofore I had experienced, not in my real and mundane life, at least not since childhood, but rather only in my nightmare. I felt an incredible sense of danger and mystery and wonder, that extraordinary feeling of enchantment and heightened awareness of one who has lived in a trivial and commonplace world and then suddenly and quite matter-of-factly stepped into something very like the supernatural. And yet, I must emphasize, it did not feel really supernatural at all. It felt vivid, true, so true I felt certain it must be the dream again, although I knew it wasn't. Every detail of that house was most vividly and perfectly that of the dream, including the furnishings, the painting of a rather sad looking beauty of the last century whom the old gentleman pointed out as his grandmother, and an unfortunate gash towards the bottom of the bannister which, stickler for detail as I must be, I had noticed many times in my dream, as it was always at the point where my hand rested as I began to move up the stairs. It was the house in my nightmare, there was no mistaking it.

I realized that my host had been speaking to me for some time without penetrating much into my consciousness, and managed to compose myself well enough to carry on some sort of conversation with him. To my disappointment, the clocks he wished to sell were not upstairs, but in a study off the hallway, a place I had only glanced into in my dream. The clocks were interesting enough, it was clear to me I would do well to buy them, although not, under other circumstances, at the prices he imagined they were worth, but my mind was not much on these transactions, and I managed finally to turn our conversation towards grandfather clocks, of which, he said, he only had the one, at the top of the staircase, there, but that he would not care to part with that one, as it was the oldest and dearest of his collection. I asked him could I please at least have a look at it, and he very kindly and with a good deal of huffing and puffing led me up the staircase, every step of which I knew by heart, until we were standing at the top of the steps, looking at my old nemesis, the grandfather clock of my dream.

The doors upstairs were all closed. I asked the old man if he lived here alone, and he replied that he had a granddaughter, a rather frail girl, not in the best of health, who seldom came downstairs, but was a great comfort to him in his old age. This seemed to remind him of some neglected duty, and before I could find a way to protest, he had ushered me down the stairs and out the door, suggesting that I call him the next day if I cared to make an offer. I found myself standing out in the street, still very much awake, and as excited as I had ever been in my life, and as frustrated. The leaves circled round me in little hysterical pirouettes as I walked home in the wind. I ended up walking for hours, I couldn't stop thinking about that house, the dream, the old man's talk about his granddaughter. I could not explain what had happened to me. I didn't want to explain it. And I didn't want to wake up. But of course, I wasn't dreaming.

The next day, in a perfect frenzy of anticipation, I called the old man, rather too early, I think, for he sounded awfully fuzzy, and made him an incredibly generous offer for his clocks, but to my horror he announced that he had changed his mind, that he could not after all part with any of them, and that he would have to find some other way to raise money, perhaps by selling some property in another part of the city. I tried to reason with him, I raised the amount to perfectly ridiculous heights, but the old man had made up his mind, and my inexplicable passion for his clocks I think began to make him suspect that one of them must be even more valuable than he had thought. The old man finally became so irritated that he virtually hung up on me, and I stood there, phone in my hand, in tears, knowing that my last legitimate connection with that magic place had vanished as quickly as it had appeared. I was in despair. I could not sleep, I could not eat. I began to call the house at various times during the day, hoping to hear the granddaughter's voice, but only the old man, or sometimes an elderly woman I took to be his rather feeble-minded housekeeper, would answer, and I would be forced to hang up, or to apologize and say wrong number, or, once, to make up an idiotic cover story about a telephone survey. I realized finally that I could no longer subject myself to such torture and indignity. I had to forget about it. But I could not forget.

One night I had the dream again, as vivid and terrible as ever, and woke up with the sound of the clock's second chime in my ears, convinced I could not let this go on any longer. I got up, got dressed, and walked to the house, a considerable distance, in the middle of the night. I don't know what I had expected to do there, but after standing in the cold and watching the house for some time, I noticed a small window near the front door, that had been partially obstructed by a large evergreen. I made my way across the yard and behind the evergreen to the window, and looked in. I could see very little, pieces of furniture in the shadows, the house still and dark. I tried the window. It opened. I stood there, the window open before me, listening to the clocks tick inside the house. I could see the black and white checkerboard floor of the entry way at the foot of the staircase. I hesitated for just a moment — I am hardly an adventurous person, even on my better days, but the force of the obsession was too great. I crawled in the window and stood there in the dark, on the checkerboard surface, looking up the stairs, the clocks ticking everywhere around me. I reached for the bannister, felt the gash in the wood there, and made my way up the staircase.

At the top of the stairs I passed the grandfather clock and noticed, with a start, that the time was just before two a.m., exactly as in the dream. Why this should have surprised me, I don't know, but it did, and it led me to fear, briefly, that my adventure would end badly. For a moment I considered going back down the stairs and running off into the night, but I couldn't. Just a few feet away from me was the closed door that had led, in the dream, to the girl's bedroom. What if it was not really her room? What if the similarity of reality to the dream should end suddenly in an indignant old man in night-cap and a screaming of sirens and humiliating police questions? What if the old man kept a gun? But I could not go back. I turned the doorknob carefully and opened the door, and there, on the canopy bed before me, lay the girl, just as in the dream. I have no idea what I was going to do when I got to her, but I could not help myself from moving towards her. I had to find out what the dream would not show me — what happened when I crossed the room to the edge of the bed and then to the sleeping girl. I moved towards the bed, and then hesitated when I had reached the point where the clock always awoke me in the dream. I was trembling, sweating horribly, my legs felt weak, but I knew I must go on, just a few more steps and I could touch her. Then the clock at the top of the stairs chimed once, twice, and to my horror I found myself back again in my own bed, sitting up, staring at the wall and thoroughly baffled and miserable. I felt I had a right to be upset. I could not understand what on earth had happened. It hardly seemed fair. I was conscious of having gotten out of bed, gone out into the cold, broken into the house — and yet, here I was, waking up in my own bed again. It was all very alarming.

I could not get back to sleep that night, and the next day I opened the shop in the most horrible mood imaginable. I had thought the whole thing through. I must in fact have dreamed I had gone to the house. But how could I make certain this did not happen again? How could I, in short, verify at any given time that I was not indeed dreaming when I thought I was awake? I spent the whole day thinking about this. I decided not to go to bed at all that night. I worked late, until after midnight, then went to the all night diner around the corner and had something to eat and drank coffee. I ran into a policeman I knew there, and could not get rid of him for some time—I was forced to listen to interminable stories about his wife's passion for antique crockery. But I was certain, absolutely certain, that I was quite awake, and had been all day. Finally I got away from the policeman and made my way across town to the house again. Everything was as before. I made my way to the window, opened it, crept into the entranceway and up the stairs. I hesitated at the doorway. I went into the room. There she lay, all as before. I knew this time I was perfectly awake, and I moved grimly towards the bed, whereupon, of course, the wretched clock in the hallway chimed twice, and I found myself once again in my bed at home. I was furious. What on earth was happening to me? Could it be that my entire day had been an incredibly extended dream within a dream? Or had I just been so tired I had forgotten coming home to bed? I thought I would go mad with frustration. But that day, at work, now twice as haggard and twice as surly to my poor customers, I realized that if I just planned carefully enough, I could subvert the dream.

That night I went back to the house, but I went earlier, around midnight. There was, unfortunately, a light burning in the girl's window, and another downstairs, and I was forced to stand out in the cold and wait until the house became at last entirely dark and still. Finally I crept to the house, crawled in the window, and stepped into the checkerboard entranceway. I went up the stairs. It was nearly two a.m. I opened the door to her room. She was sleeping there, as before. It seemed to me that if I could just do something to change the dream, to stop it, alter it, subvert it somehow, that I could conquer it, move it finally to its proper conclusion in reality. I stood there watching her sleep, her breasts rising and falling gently in her nightgown as she slept. Mechanically I began to move towards her, but at the last moment I somehow found the strength to turn and bolt back into the hallway and open the face of the clock — it was just about to strike. But in my haste I tripped over the rug, grabbed onto the clock to support myself, overbalanced, the clock in my arms, and fell backwards down the staircase with the heavy clock on top of me. The next thing I remember is lying there at the bottom of the steps, the clock still in my arms, on top of me, with a kind of chilling numbness spreading through my body and seemingly eating up the pain along my back and neck. I remember seeing the door at the top of the stairs open, and the girl come out timidly to the edge of the staircase to look down. She looked so small and frail and beautiful there at the top of the steps, looking down at me in her white nightgown, so close and yet so infinitely, impossibly far away from me. Then her image began to blur and the last thing I heard, as I died, was the loud relentless chiming of the clock, once, twice, as it lay heavily upon me — right on time, of course.

I woke up in my bed at home, quite unharmed, but supremely unhappy, and yet not. For I had managed an extraordinary thing. I had managed to change the outcome — not the ultimate outcome, of course, but at least the events leading up to the penultimate outcome, as it were. By sheer force of will I had somehow managed to alter the nightmare, just a bit, just for a moment. I had made her see me. She had seen me. She had looked into my eyes.

It had been of course terribly humiliating, lying there at the bottom of the steps, a ridiculous intruder with a grandfather clock on top of him, lying broken-backed and dying there below her, but at least through that humiliation, that will to follow one's obsession, I had at least made her see me, I was someone she could never forget then, you see?

But of course she has forgotten me. Or, rather, she has nothing really to forget, for it only happened in my nightmare, as it must have been, a nightmare, for I am here, now, speaking, apparently whole, and she is there, no doubt, sleeping quietly.

Do you know what I wonder? I wonder what she is dreaming about there, in that house, every night. Could it be, could it be that she is dreaming about me? Could it be that each night when she sleeps she dreams of an obsessed man coming up the steps to her room, does she dream him into her room, and then, just when he is about to touch her, does the clock strike for her also, and does she awaken to find no one there? Did her dream change because I managed to change mine once? Did she dream me there dead at the bottom of the stairs? Perhaps if one is just obsessed enough, one can create some sort of desperate interpenetration of nightmares, something very like, very like a kind of intimacy, do you think?

Then again, perhaps she doesn't dream at all. Perhaps she dreams of someone quite different. Or perhaps she isn't even there. I don't know. I am by nature, you see, an obsessive man, and this is an obsession I fear I shall never be able to awaken from. It's almost time now. I don't want to be late. It's rather cold tonight. (*He is putting on his coat and hat.*) I will go to the house and try again. Tonight I'm going to try and stop the clock before I get to the room, and set it back a ways, so I can have a bit more time with her. The problem is, I'm not sure I can resist opening the door when I get to the top of the stairs, and once I've gone in and seen her, I'm not sure I can make myself get back out into the hallway again in time to stop it. It's hard to say what I will do. But I must try, after all. I mean, if one does not carefully nurture and cherish one's obsession, what else has one? (*He goes to the door, stops, listens to the clocks tick.*) Listen to them. It's a kind of music, isn't it? One only has, after all, so much time, you know.

(*He goes out. The sound of many ticking clocks. Lights fade and out.*)

Captain Cook

There is one character, Elizabeth, an attractive woman of perhaps 30. She is alone on a bare stage with four wooden chairs.

Captain James Cook (1728–1779) made three famous exploratory voyages to the South Pacific between 1768 and 1779, mapping New Zealand, sailing for the first time south across the Antarctic Circle, landing on the western coast of North America, and discovering the Sandwich Islands, now called Hawaii, where he was killed after going ashore to recover a small boat stolen by a Hawaiian. At Kealakekua Bay, where he died, there is a bronze tablet reading

NEAR THIS SPOT
CAPT. JAMES COOK
WAS KILLED
FEBRUARY 14, 1779.

His widow in England survived him by some years.

"The heart of another is a dark forest."
— Turgenev

Captain Cook

(Lights up slowly on ELIZABETH.)

ELIZABETH. After my husband's death, they gave me a trunk, the contents of which I shall now enumerate. One Bible, Holy, containing the Old and New Testaments, much read, Oxford, M. Baskett, 1765, illustrated, with my husband's bookplate, used by him in conducting divine service on board the Resolution, his very leaky ship. One cabin tea caddy, a wooden box, four and a half inches high by seven deep, of cedar veneer on pine inlaid with walnut and other timbers. Two compartments inside with cedar lids and ivory knobs. One memorial ring, the design made from my husband's hair, with inscription, Captain James Cook, 14 February 1779. On an accompanying envelope, written in ink. For His Widow. Odd word, that. Widow. It's a spidery word. Vaguely poisonous. Said the Widow Cook.

The fact is, you know, he was a stupid man, a stupid, hateful man, with the strongest hands, and the kindest, most wicked eyes. Once he came home with this, this impossible thing, this utterly impossible thing, and I asked him what it was, and he replied, with a perfectly straight face, This is my astrolabe. It's not anything of the kind, I replied, what a horrible thing to say to your wife. It is, he said. Although now of course we employ a reflecting or bubble sextant. And then he offered to show me his sextant. He was always teasing me. How could one tell when he was teasing and when he was not? And then he would go away. Charm me, seduce me, impregnate me repeatedly, then kiss me goodbye and disappear in a boat for years and years at a time. A perfectly monstrous man. So gentle with me. Out among the savages. In the southern parts. Where it is beastly hot.

But when you go far enough south, he would say, when you go far enough south, then it gradually begins actually to grow colder, it gets very cold, until, when you are as far south as you can go, everything is very white and still, and you look up into the air, and you fall into the air, at the bottom of the world, you look up and fall into the air, and you never come back.

I extract certain objects from a trunk and this is supposed to make a kind of sense out of things. Artifacts. The ship on the sea is the soul lost in an ocean of loneliness. In the land of the cannibals, exploration and discovery, this entails of course a certain amount of murder, one pays a price, but if there were no exploration, how then would there be discovery, how would the soul grow? The world waits there like a mouth that swallows him, he sails into it with these dirty ignorant souls on frail wooden structures looking for truth and finding something somewhat less. My brain is full of useless correspondences. God returns as Jesus and is nailed to a piece of wood. My husband returns as a god and the islanders butcher him. Moral—if God leaves the room he had damn well better not come back. We always kill our gods.

He was an imperfect god. Mr Ledyard asserts that Captain Cook was often more influenced by acquiring a hog from the natives than the honor of always being nice in the distribution of justice impartially. Food was scarce. He was often severe with them. The full exertion of extreme power is an argument of extreme weakness, and nature seemed to inform the insulted natives of the truth of this maxim, by the manifestation of their subsequent resentments. So says Mr Ledyard, who unfortunately was not himself butchered by them, which much improved his natural sympathy for natives in general. One knows that one is very good at something when one can feel the waves of envy and hatred rolling back towards one like an ocean, from all sides. And yet Mr Ledyard worshipped him as much as anyone. They all worshipped him.

His best friends, Captain Clerke and Doctor Anderson, would sit on the deck, watching the gulls, knowing they would not be able to stand the cold this time, they would talk of staying on in Tahiti, stringing out their poor consumptive lives a few more years in paradise, and my husband would have let them, for he was always humane with his men, and they were no good to him dead, but Mr Clerke would be silent for the longest time and then comment finally to Doctor Anderson that he was afraid he would not be able to get his papers and accounts in order by the time they left Tahiti, and so it would go, at each warm stop, until they were too far out in the cold, watching the gulls, the sea taking small bites out of their lungs. Men followed Captain Cook even unto death.

Saint Thomas Aquinas asks whether a man who has eaten nothing but human flesh all his life could be resurrected? Would his victims be deprived of their bodies on judgement day? And, if not, then what would make up his own body? Of course, how many cannibals are likely to go to heaven? Yet God lives there, and his cannibalism is a well-documented fact, as in the communion service, so there is some hope, after all, I suppose.

One carved ditty box shaped like a coffin, on a silver stand, containing a rough watercolor sketch of the death of Cook, with a lock of his hair and a document of identification, with the inscription, Made of Resolution Oak for Mrs Cook by the Crew. Inset in lid are two silver plates inscribed, Quebec, Newfoundland, Greenwich, Australia, and Lono and the Seaman's Idol. Inset at bottom of third silver plate inscribed, Captain James Cook, Slain at Owyhee, 14 February, 1779.

He should not have gone, of course. The Resolution was a ship still in her prime, so insisted Lord Sandwich. My husband said she looked fine to one who would get to spend the voyage home in bed in England. Lord Sandwich, devouring roasted fowl, laughed and belched and tried to think up a way to eat meat without getting his fingers so greasy. My husband was very tired, he wanted to rest, to stay home with his lovely wife, to teach, to read, to write, to take walks on the land. He had lost the land, do you see? He had been out there so long, he had lost his feeling for the land. Roseberry Topping on Cleveland hills. Rubbish, nonsense, stuff and poppyshit, said Lord Sandwich. You're going and that's that. Have some of this damned chicken, he said, but save the ass for your betters, the part that goeth over the wall last is the only part for the upper class. Do you think, he said, if I stuck this between two slices of bread, it might not grease my damned fingers so? But Captain Cook did not answer.

If I return safely in the Resolution, said John Gore, the next trip I may safely venture in a ship built of gingerbread. He was a good fellow, we had him to dinner, an American, he got them kangaroo meat and stingray in Australia. There were other men. Clerke was a farmer's son from Essex, always cheerful, making us laugh at table, he went with my husband on all his voyages, a brave man, a kind man, a dead man.

This day, said Rickman's journal, the gentlemen in the gunroom dined on a frickassee of rats, which they accounted a venison feast, and it was a high treat to the sailors, whenever they could be lucky enough to catch a number sufficient enough to make a meal.

Short eyes, said the Hawaiian, long eyes, walking about in the rain, earthquake and whirlwind, seabird and trickle of blood, tongue of the god wags in my dreams, above the cold altar, there are savages in my dreams, maneater, caterpillar, rolling of eyes and thrusting of tongue, upland and mountain, and low lying island, my flesh, god with a mouth full of maggots, roseberry topping on cleveland hills.

One clock, of dark wood and glass case, with handle at the top, nineteen inches high, face plain, but with gilt decoration, there is gilt and there is guilt, one is gold and the other is black, and an inscription of brass reading, This clock belonged to Captain James Cook the navigator and made the voyage round the world with him in 1779. The clock did. I did not. Said the widow Cook.

Then there was the business of Riou's dog. Where is my dog, he said, what's become of my dog, and the men there eating, asked him, what? Got a bug up yer drawers? And Riou asks again, where is his dog, the New Zealand dog he had stolen from the cannibals, the dog that bit Mr Rickman and Mr Home, and Mr Burney, is that the dog you means, Neddy? And yes, Riou says, be the dog ill tempered or not, it is a present I am bringing home to my patroness, the Marchioness of Townsend. So Mr Home pulls out a furry, gore-stained thing and tosses it over Mr Riou's head, and Riou, gagging and retching in disgust, pulls it from his face and realizes it is the skin of his dog. My dog, he screams, you have skinned my dog. Don't get upset, Neddy, they say, it ain't good for yer delicate constitution, what would the Marchioness of Townsend think? And they explain—

Well, you see, Neddy, your dog having come from the

cannibal isles, and being a bit of a cannibal himself, considering the substantial bites he took out of several of us, we felt, while you was on shore duty, we ought to take the offending party in and have a proper court martial, and I'm sorry to say it went against the dog in the decision, you see, and the sentence of death was duly carried out, and since the punishment ought to fit the crime, and seeing as how we was each of us hungry enough to eat a horse behind the saddle, we et him.

My god, says Riou, you're nothing but a bunch of bloody cannibals. This is detestable. And he goes off sulking, and the others continue to eat, and then, after a bit, Mr Riou comes back. Damn you, he says, did you not even have the decency to leave me a share of it? And Mr Home calmly reaches under the table and pulls out a dish of meat. That I did, Neddy me boy, he says, and here it is for you. Whereupon Mr Riou damns the barbarians to hell, and then sits down and begins to eat with them. Good, ain't it? says Mr Home. Yes. It is. It is good.

There are seagulls. Clerke is working at his desk. Anderson is watching the gulls. They are leaving tomorrow. But Mr Clerke says all his papers and affairs are still not in order. But they may stay at the next fine island, with beautiful native women, and water. They shall get off there, if that is agreeable to Mr Anderson, who coughs and says it is. It would be a great waste, says Dr Anderson, to lose twenty or thirty years of one's life, that need not be wasted. And Mr Clerke agrees. To die for nothing would be a very great waste, in the great cold of the south sea, a very great waste. Mr Clerke agrees and goes back to his papers, and Dr Anderson watches the gulls, and my husband looks at them and says nothing at all.

Two young officers, Burney and Phillips, by moonlight. A bit aching for the women are you, Mr Burney?

And aren't you? asks Burney back to him. Between islands, yes. But I mean civilized women, says Burney. I
didn't know there were any civilized women, says Mr
Phillips, who will subsequently marry Burney's sister
and make her terribly unhappy. I mean the companionship, says Burney. In the South Sea Islands, I must tell
you, the young girls are slim, and they have long soft hair,
and large dark eyes, and they sit bare-breasted by the
water and smile shyly at you.

No, says Mr Phillips, I don't mean for the companionship, I mean for the wet red mouth between their fine
white thighs. For companionship I'll have a dog, thank
you. These are sailors, of course. And sailors are men.
And men are cannibals. And my husband was a man.
And no doubt he also missed me. Perhaps for the
companionship.

And finally Dr Anderson gets fed up, and he says,
Charlie Clerke, I see we've been a month here as close to
paradise as any tubercular son of a bitches will ever get,
yet you still find that you've not yet finished piddling
with your bloody wretched papers and affairs, and we
must head south again when the ship goes, further into
the cold that will kill us both, that's what I see, you
bloody damned blockhead, and I don't like it a bit. And
Captain Clerke, who is a very gentle soul, and afraid of
no man on earth, smiles sadly at his friend Dr Anderson,
and says nothing, and puts his hand for a moment on his
shoulder, and then goes back to his work. And Anderson
looks at him and says quietly, You're going to stick with
Captain Cook until it's killed you, aren't you? And Mr
Clerke says, Do you know, I have always been fascinated
by seagulls. I think I shall never tire of watching them
and listening to them. Most sailors hate them, I know,
but I find them strangely compelling, their triumphs and

their quarrels and tragedies. Don't you? No, says Anderson. No, I don't. And he watches the gulls. He will stay with my husband also, and die in the cold, coughing up blood into a handkerchief.

And young Mr Burney asks Captain Cook my husband if they are putting in at so and so island, and Captain Cook my husband says yes, and young Mr Burney begs pardon to wonder about Mr Clerke and Dr Anderson, who have been planning for some time to resign their commissions and remain in these islands, because of the consumption. So? asks my husband. So, sir, says young Mr Burney, so and so island is the last chance for them, sir, for even if we were to come across habitable islands to the south, we would be unfamiliar with the natives, and it would be inadvisable to leave them in the company of natives we did not trust.

And my husband says, Mr Burney, I have things to do, if you've got something to do, please go about your business. I've given them permission to resign and remain wherever they please.

I know that, sir, says Burney, but Mr Clerke keeps finding excuses to stay on, and I thought that, if possible, you might — Look here, Mr Burney, interrupts my husband, I can't very well throw Mr Clerke bodily off the ship, now, can I? No sir, says Burney, but you could make an effort to remove some of his excuses, sir, that is, if you could, rather, um, assume that he is leaving, and, um — Mr Burney, says my husband, you are quite out of order. They'll die in the cold, Captain, says young Mr Burney, forgetting himself. We're killing them. I am not killing them, said Captain Cook. The cold will kill them, says Mr Burney. Sir. There is a pause. The sound of gulls. You might consider, Mr Burney, says my husband, that it is in most cases neither possible nor desirable to change a man's behavior by taking him for either more or less than what he takes himself to be. Each of us charts his own voyage, to whatever destination. Do you understand that? No sir, says Mr Burney. No, of course he doesn't. I will do what I can, says my husband. But before he gets a chance to, he will himself have reached his own charted destination.

A collection of fifty specimens of bark cloth, feathers of small birds, hair of natives, twine, etcetera, as collected on the different voyages of Captain Cook to the South sea.

At night I dream of a Hawaiian man. He is speaking to my husband. This is what he says. You see a lot, Cook. You see that we are people, that we bleed like you, love and hate like you. You try and save us from the diseases your sailors bring, from their violence, from ourselves. You even love us, Cook, some of us, not the way your crews do, but in your gentle way, not selfish. You are mostly a good man, sir, and there will never be such a fine Captain in the world again as you are, you give us your love when you can, and our lives when you can, you treat us like your children, Cook. And that is the heart of the matter.

We are not your children. The only power you have over us is what we give you, and we have chosen to take back what we have given, because we gave it when we mistook you for our father, and you did not refuse it. But then we touched you, and saw that you were made of flesh, and you were our friend as an adult is friend to a child. You kept your grown man's dignity but would not allow us ours. Either we are all grown men, or we are all children. You saw that our lives were human lives, but

you allowed us dignity only as children. And no matter
how much you have loved us, or we have loved you, we
are not your children. And that is why we must kill you.
We thought you were a god returned and we were mistaken. We thought you were our fate, but we are yours.

Sanderson, grocer and haberdasher, said the box. And
always the sea beside, clutching, taking small bites.

Anything may be a god. Even a corpse. Everything has
potentially some god lurking inside it, waiting to sink its
teeth into our necks. The gods come to visit us. Sometimes they come disguised as men. God rises up and he is
the morning. She leans down and is the afternoon.
Everything passes through the woman, her body and her
soul. The God Lono lives in the waters, is the clouds and
storms, places the stars that sail in the dark, his signs are
lightning and thunder, dark clouds, rainbows, wind and
rain, earthquakes and waterspouts. In the rainy season
festival the people stop their work, play games and mate.
We light fires on the beach. We bathe naked in the ocean.
We blindfold the priest, we fight and collect offerings.
We take a man's eye. The new year begins.

Lono sends out his brothers to find him a wife, and
they go from island to island, I also live upon an island, I
know of islands, and they find a beautiful woman in a
breadfruit grove surrounded by many birds. He makes
her his wife, and she becomes a goddess, he has de-
scended upon a rainbow, and they live at Kealakekua,
where my husband died, and when he fears she has betrayed him, he beats her to death in anger. But she is
innocent. Then Lono travels about the island like a
madman, and disappears into the water, but promises to
return sailing an island shaded with trees, like my husband's ship with its masts and sails, swarming with fowl
and swine, as my husband's ship was. So you see, he was

the god, when he came to them. For a moment. And then, like all gods, he was killed by his worshippers.

The worst of the nightmares is this, like a series of pictures moving, no sound, except for a hideous flapping, batlike noise, the picture is unsteady, there are a crowd of natives, many with sticks and rocks, some with knives and spears, and in the midst of them a tall, powerfully built man of perhaps fifty, dressed as an English sea-captain. He has a gun in one hand, and on the beach are two or three wounded sailors amidst the swarming natives. The tall man is my husband. He seems to be gesturing to someone just out of the picture, just off the shore in the sea, he seems neither angry nor afraid, only inpatient, irritated. Now he has turned his back and is gesturing towards the sea, and then back to the natives, and then back to the sea, and there is one particular native, I see his face very clearly, he lunges, driving something long and sharp into my husband's back. My husband stands quite motionless, his face unreadable, then his arms swing outward and he falls towards me into the water at the shore's edge, his eyes and the clutch of his hands. The natives drag the body from the sea and repeatedly stab it. The body is lost in an ocean of flesh and then there is only whiteness and the horrible batlike flapping sound. This is my nightmare, said the little wife, said the widow Cook, almost done now.

It is the opinion of the very angry Mr King that all the natives should be killed. Ungrateful, vicious children, animals, he calls them. Butchers, cannibals, judases. Bring the ships around, says Mr King, and level the cannons at the villages, and blow them all to bloody hell, then land and burn and slaughter every last one of the useless buggars, cut them to pieces as they did to him, cut open the wombs of their women, destroy them utterly.

Captain Clerke waits quietly for Mr King to calm himself. Mr King is crying. Then, gently, he asks, Now, Mr King, what shall we really do to these people?

Nothing, says Mr King. Nothing at all. Let them be. Just let them be.

And that is what they do. And before they sail, the natives send them a present, in a little box. It is a large piece of meat, of raw, newly butchered meat. It is a part of my husband's thigh. The rest of him they have eaten.

Of other objects I have these: a chart, showing the Western Hemisphere, embroidered in silk by Mrs James Cook, showing the tracks of her husband, Captain Cook, from 1769 to 1779.

A cup, said to be the communion cup used by Captain Cook, in its leather case.

Various nautical instruments for chart work.

A necklet of Mrs Cook's hair, forty three inches long, which Captain Cook took on his last voyage.

When you travel too far south, and it begins to be cold again, you reach the place, you reach the place —

I was not your child. I had a life too. You had no right. You had no right.

I have these fragments, you see.

Well, it is time for my supper. I must go and eat. I forget why.

Tonight we are having lamb, I think.

(*She stands there. Fade to darkness.*)

The Girlhood of Shakespeare's Heroines

Five plays by

Don Nigro

Dead Men's Fingers
Axis Sally
How Many Children Had Lady Macbeth?
Notes From The Moated Grange
Full Fathom Five

The Girlhood of Shakespeare's Heroines was first produced by the Porthouse Theatre Company in the Wright-Curtis Theatre on the campus of Kent State University in Kent, Ohio in July and August, 1988, with the following cast:

Dead Men's Fingers
OPHELIA .... Gretchen Claggett
   Axis Sally
ZOE .... Kristin Kundert
   How Many Children Had Lady Macbeth?
BONNIE .... Kerry Shanklin
   Notes From the Moated Grange
MARIANA .... Amy Jorgensen
   Full Fathom Five
MIRANDA .... Alicia Rene Washington

The production was directed by Marya Bednerik.
Scene and Lighting Design by Ralph Dressler.
Costume Design by Estelle Painter.
Stage Manager, Scott Patrick Cronin-Campbell.

Notes

Five acts in a Shakespeare play. Here, five plays make one interconnected play. The juxtaposition of each to each of the others multiplies the images, as in a hall of mirrors. Hamlet's advice to the players was to hold the mirror up to nature. 'All the world's a stage,' Jaques says. The Globe was the little world upon which Shakespeare strutted and fretted. He was the god of his world, like Prospero on his island, or God in the Garden of Eden. Creators, all. All theatres are the same theatre.

One primary way a man attempts to understand the world he is cast in is through the complex series of relations he appears to have with the sequence of significant women in his life. Each is her own separate self but also in his mind the anima he carries within him, projected outwards upon her. This is, of course, unfair. Love is merely a madness. All projection distorts. The beloved is made of ambiguity. Each is a mystery, a piece of the puzzle, a fragment of broken mirror.

The theatre is a mirror, like the face of the beloved. The stage is a magic figure drawn, within which all times and places imaginable coexist, waiting to be conjured. The greatest act of love is to pay attention. The theatre is a place where we go to pay attention to a universe drawn in miniature. We look in the mirror, as through a glass darkly, to see ourselves.

Each of the five parts of this play is a play in itself, meant to stand alone as such. But when the five are done together they become one play, and must be done in the order in which they appear here. The title of each play is significant and must be listed in the program as a part of the cast of characters.

The portraits of Ophelia and Mariana by John Everett Millais can be found in Timothy Hilton's *The Pre-Raphaelites*, (London, Thames and Hudson, 1970) pages 76 and 64.

Axis Sally died in Columbus in 1988, a week before the first production of this play began rehearsal.

When done as one play, the transitions are part of the play, the actresses perhaps remain to watch, become spectators in the dark, empty theatre, there must be no empty spaces between scenes, everything connects, all interconnections strengthen, no blackouts. The way the play moves is always a part of the play.

Dead Men's Fingers

Dead Men's Fingers

(*On a bare stage, OPHELIA, with flowers, in a tattered dress, very beautiful, looking much as she does in the painting by John Everett Millais.*)

OPHELIA. It's very strange, not what I had expected it to be. I don't know what I expected, exactly, but this definitely isn't it. And yet it seems, in the end, to have been more or less inevitable that this is what it should have turned out, finally, to be like. Remembrance. Death is remembrance. As of a performance. As of a play completed. In a dark, empty theatre. Do you know what I keep thinking of? I keep thinking of poor old Yorick, of all things, Yorick and his impossibly stupid and vulgar jokes. What a silly thing. And yet, when I try to reconstruct my childhood, I simply can't stop thinking of him, of drunken, pathetic old Yorick, telling stories. Yorick told perhaps the worst stories in the entire history of jesterdom. There was one, I remember, about somebody pouring poison in the porches of somebody's ears. I remember looking over at the King's brother, Claudius, and seeing that he was not laughing, and wondering what he was thinking about. I'll tell you one of Yorick's stories, if you like — they're awfully stupid, but they have a certain clumsy charm. My favorite was always the one about the unfortunate Frenchman in Wales. Ready? All right, I shall endeavor not to ballocks this up too badly. So. A certain Frenchman goeth into Wales, and he do stoppeth at a house which he mistaketh for an country inn, desiring much a breakfast of eggs. But the old woman of the house speaketh only Welsh, and knoweth not what the French fellow means. And the fellow, grown extremely frustrate and hungry, for he had tra-

67

velled in the rain all night, having lost his horse and his way in the mud, and much desiring eggs, finally beginneth, in his desperate hunger, to illustrate his desire to the old woman by clucking like a chicken, to put his hands under his armpits and strut, clucking and bucking as a chicken is want to do, and at this the old Welsh woman, having never before met with a Frenchman, beginneth to fear for the gentleman's sanity, and the French fellow, mistaking her extremely cautious attitude towards him as the beginning of international communication, he clucketh more loudly yet, and commenceth to go through the motions of laying an egg, and as the French gentleman reacheth behind himself and pretendeth to pull out an egg, with a loud squawk, from his lower hole, to his great delight and the old woman's greater alarm, and then to offer it to her, and to pretendeth that he was eating it with great relish, and the old Welsh woman could stand this no longer, and does thus begin to scream and run madly away, and the French gentleman, knowing not what else to do, and being very hungry, and a persistent fellow by nature, followeth her still in the manner of a chicken, attempting to make her understand, and then the villagers, being roused from their work by the old woman's shrieking, and seeing her pursued by a lunatic, did throw a fishing net over the poor French gentleman, and did drag him off, with much swearing and struggling in a language which seemed to them gibberish, and depositeth him in a Welsh madhouse, where the unfortunate man resideth to this day. Not much of a story, I will admit. And yet I cannot forget it, or Yorick's droll and dogged way of telling it, for I heard it so many times that, like a multitude of trivial or foolish things in our childhood, it came to mean something more than had been originally intended, especially as I began to feel, more and more as I grew older, much like that unfortunate French gentleman, desperate to communicate my needs, but speaking, as it were, to a race of persons entirely ignorant of my native language, and thus doomed to misinterpret everything I say and do. My identification with this poor Frenchman is now nearly complete, but it did not occur to me until much later that perhaps the reason old Yorick so insisted upon telling it over and over was that in some mysterious way he, too, identified with the French gentleman, that his occupation of jester was rather like the poor man's chicken imitation, like being trapped in a ridiculous suit of clothing one could not escape from, rather like a chastity belt. So you see, Yorick and the Frenchman who desired a breakfast of eggs and I have a great deal more in common than one might at first expect. These things come at me, moments, like fragments of truth, written in obscure languages. Here's another one: We're very small, playing in the garden, under the crab apple tree, Hamlet, Laertes and me. Hamlet suggests that we play Adam and Eve in the Garden of Eden. Hamlet's games, even then, always seemed to take the form of elaborate stage plays, with himself as director, god and star. First, he says, Laertes and I must take off all our clothing. I have some reservations about this, but in the end we always do everything Hamlet tells us to. Now, says Hamlet, Laertes is Adam and Ophelia is Eve. But she's my sister, protests Laertes. So was Eve Adam's sister, says Hamlet. They had the same father, didn't they? Oh, says Laertes. He was never very bright. Now, says Hamlet, I am the serpent, and Laertes must go away and name some animals. Which animals? asks Laertes. I can't say, answers Hamlet reasonably, until you've named them, can I? So Laertes goes off sulking to find some animals to name. We have no animals in Denmark, he says, kicking the dirt and bruising the knuckles of his toes. When Laertes is gone, Hamlet turns to me and says, Hello, Eve. I'm the serpent. I don't like serpents. I say. Oh, but you must like me, he says, I'm a very nice serpent. I've come to bring you knowledge. What knowledge? I ask, very suspicious, and beginning to get cold, standing there naked in the garden. Knowledge, says Hamlet, of good and evil. And then he pulls me towards him, and he kisses me, and puts his tongue in my mouth. What on earth are you doing? I ask, pulling away. I'm being a serpent, he says. Serpent tongues do that. Not in my mouth, they don't, I say. Tell me about good and evil. Well, he says — but before he can tell me, my father catches us, and I get a good whipping. Hamlet, of course, gets off with a tongue lashing from the old King, who is rather amused by the whole thing. This by the way was the pattern of our youth, Hamlet would get other people in trouble and then somehow evade responsibility for it. I always regretted not getting from him the answer about good and evil, it was an important question for me. But my misfortune was that, although I thought much about such things, I tended to keep them to myself, and thus I perpetuated the myth that I was beautiful but not very bright. The fact is, I am, and have always been, much too intelligent for my own good — it was I think my downfall, in fact, that I could think, and think much more deeply and efficiently than that poor spoiled delinquent Hamlet ever could, but there was a kind of blindness all about me, they could not see it, would not see it, for along with my intelligence came a desire to be thought good, to be kind to those around me, to give my father what pleasure I could, to keep my brother Laertes, who was in his own way even stupider than my dear moronic father,

as serene from moment to moment as could be expected
— my tragedy was that while I loved all these people I
knew how stupid they were, and could do nothing about
it. So I did my chicken act and they spoke Welsh. And
gradually I began to go insane. It was not, as some have
thought, a direct result of my father's murder. Oh, no,
no, such things only give us an excuse to manifest the
madness that is already within us. No, the madness
began in my childhood, it was the result of my attempts
to solve the mystery of the knowledge of the tree of good
and evil—I could make no sense of it. For everything
around me seemed such a terrible admixture of things
partly lovely and partly horrid. Hamlet was kind and
funny and utterly charming and yet cruel and selfish and
cold and full of hatred. The Queen was beautiful and
kind and gentle and considerate and also blind and foolish and vain and weak. Claudius was ambitious and deceitful and a murderer, but he was also rather more intelligent than the others, well read, a gifted painter, a person
who could discuss botany or point out the constellations
or recall the name of a poor tailor he had met in the street
twelve years ago and ask him about his three children
and his wife with the glass eye. He was in many ways a
better king than the brother he murdered. And he loved
Gertrude with all his heart. He felt that Hamlet was
mentally ill and very dangerous, and he was right on both
counts. And Laertes loved me with great apparent devo-
tion, but Hamlet's remark about eating a crocodile at my
shabby burial service was, I'm sorry to say, much to the
point, for in fact I believe Laertes loved the idea of having
a sister more than he loved me in particular — in reality I
believe his actual attachment to me was more sexual
than anything else, he desired me, physically desired me,
at least from the day Hamlet cast us as Adam and Eve in

the garden. And then there is Father, my dear father, who often spoke words of great wisdom without, unfortunately, listening to what he was saying, who would give wise counsel mixed with absolute rubbish and never be able to tell the difference, whose love for me I found genuine and touching at one moment, only to be in the next moment utterly forgotten in a storm of peevishness. They were all such jumbles of contradictions, they made me so angry and confused, I could not deal with one of them in a consecutive way, each time I walked into a room and found one, I had to hold back, to wait and see what face they had put on this day, when what I wanted was to run at them and desperately put my arms around them and hug them, yes, even Claudius or the old dead King, hug them and tell them how hopelessly I loved them, and how fervently I hated them, but it was no use, I could do neither, it would have fallen dead upon their ears, as dead as French chicken language among the Welsh. Now, Yorick, however, Yorick, I sometimes felt, did understand this, or at least some of this, and me, or at least some of me, and much else, perhaps, but Yorick was always drunk, and then he went and fell off the battlements in a stupor one dark night and broke his neck and my heart, and there I was, still a child, and with no one to talk to for the rest of my life. It was one manifestation of my madness, I think, early on, that I would from time to time speak with Yorick, after a fashion, subsequent to his swan dive from the south tower. He would appear to me and I would speak with him, although I could never quite make out what he was saying to me, as he seemed to be speaking under water with a great wad of hay in his mouth. At any rate it was thus to Yorick's probably imaginary ghost that I confided the fact — and only to him — that I was carrying a child in my body. In a way it had all been Yorick's fault, for we had, as small children, once spied upon him engaging in a spirited act of intercourse with a young serving maid, what was her name? Gretel?

What a sight it was, let me tell you, old Yorick on top of this very young girl with very large breasts, both of them as naked as slugs, him driving, driving into her, lord, lord, we couldn't take our eyes off them, at first, but then Hamlet did a characteristic thing, he turned away in disgust, but not me, not me, I watched to the bitter end, in utter fascination, until she had ceased her whimpering and squealing and he had groaned like a dying horse, and then, and then, he pulled it out of her, and lay panting on one side, and oh, the thing, the thing, the mysterious horrible thing, lay there all wet and greasy and flabbed like a dead snake, oh, the slime on the thing, how ugly it was, and yet—. The girl lay there naked like an old painting, she was really quite beautiful, and she touched her face to his shoulder so easily, as if it had all been carefully choreographed, as if God had taught her how to do this before he allowed her to be born, and I wondered if I also knew, if I had her secret knowledge, and if Hamlet had his as well. And so it was that, some years later, with him suffering, suffering, for the death of his father the old King, and the infidelity of his mother the Queen, and the treachery of his uncle the new King, him so sad, so sad and troubled, and I was going past his chamber, one night I couldn't sleep, and I heard him crying, crying like a baby, him, who I'd never seen cry in his life, not for any amount of pain, not when he broke his arm or when Yorick died or when his father died, even, but then, months after, there, in his room, crying and crying, as if his heart would break, and so I crept in, in the dark, it was very dark and cool in his chamber, and I took off my nightgown, let it slip to the floor, and slipped quietly into his bed, he was naked, too, and so cold, and I knew how, just as Gretel the servant girl had known, God had taught me how and I had forgotten until it became necessary, and there we made the beast together, Hamlet and I, him desperate, me serene, very serene, with the ghost of the old King watching us in the dark, his two red eyes glowing in the blackness, it was after this that he turned on me and began to hate me, what do you think that nunnery business was really all about, you fools? It was his guilt, his horrible stupid guilt for it, and his anger at me for my compassion, and because I felt no guilt at all, so I could not very well tell him, could I, that I was carrying his child, and so, in the course of time, after he had conveniently murdered my poor idiot of a father, there was nothing left, I could tell, nothing left but to let the madness come gushing out like a freshwater spring, and take a swim in it. There was a willow grown aslant a brook. Actually I think it was a pond, the Queen was not a stickler for precise definitions, even in her better days. And so I did. Billowed up. Feeling the cool water creep up my legs and thighs and into my body like a snake to caress my child inside, with genuine sexual pleasure, I sang, I sang, and then, and then, gradually, up came the water to my breasts, to touch my breasts, then over my shoulders and up my neck, I shuddered and slid under, so gently, so gently under the cold water, and the dumb Queen watched and did nothing. I had entered into a deeper reality. Do you know why that poor boobie Hamlet loved the players so? Because they made alternative realities. He was not fond of the reality he'd been cast in by time or chance or the great maniacal playwright diety. He was a fool. Much more than Yorick was. I, on the other hand, played out my part to the end. Am I to be succour, or am I to be innocence? This is the heroine's dilemma. But I of course was both and neither. He touched my breasts. I thought I would die with pleasure when he touched my breasts. It's so sad he couldn't appreciate the beauty of it. The beauty in the entire pattern of it. The whole labyrinth as it is traced. The entire play one is cast in, so to speak. I suppose his play was about him not wanting to be in his play. But I had my own play, and it turned out rather well, actually, when seen from the larger point of view that madness or diety affords. That's the beauty of having the privilege of playing a character in one of the myriad of interconnected playlets in the vast dramatic epic cycle which is God's megadrama. You get to be at once vividly and inevitably the person you are cast as, but also, if you are, like me, also rather more clever than the usual player, you get, in another part of your mind, to sense the beauty of the moving action of the play that you are a character in, and of the wondrous intricacy of that play's relation to the larger set of plays with which it is simultaneously being performed. How terrible it is, and how complex and strangely beautiful, as I was saying only the other century to Yorick's ghost, with whom I and my dead child live quite happily as spectators in the dark auditorium, as all ghosts are. And so, there I am, you see. A bit of rue. A bit of rosemary. Some pansies for thoughts. Death is remembrance, a kind of quiet theatre. And there, in the pond, hung all about, I can still see them, dipping into the water, all about me, mysterious and lovely, I see dead men's fingers.

(*The light fades on her and goes out.*)

Axis Sally

Axis Sally

*(There is one character, ZOE, a pretty young woman in
her late twenties. On a bare stage she speaks to the
audience.)*

ZOE. I met her at a summer Shakespeare workshop at
Ohio State several years ago. I was only nineteen. My
husband and I had been married about a year, and I was
beginning to feel trapped and bored, and I'd always en-
joyed acting, and loved Shakespeare, so I worked up my
courage and signed up for this workshop. I was terrified
— some of the people had had much more experience
than me, and I went there the first day not knowing what
to expect. There was an old woman sitting beside me, the
most unlikely looking person to find sitting in a chalky
modern classroom on a summer day that one could
imagine. She appeared to be somewhere between sixty
and seventy, with very white hair, lots of it, done up high
on her head, her face very tanned, with upturned nose
and pursed down onion lips, and very ruddy cheeks. The
contrast between her leathery face and all that white hair
was striking, and she reminded me a bit of the old aunt
with the Siamese cats whose picture Jim Dear and Dar-
ling kept in the basement behind the furnace until she
came to visit in the old Disney movie — she wore black
Victorian skirts and white lace blouses with high, frilled
collars and long sleeves. Her shoes were black and
pointed. She was always immaculate, smelling of
powder and an incredible amount of perfume, the odor
of her perfume preceded her into rooms and followed her
down corridors like the shadow of death. She must have
seen what a frightened little thing I was, for she leaned
over to me and in a kind of mock stage whisper enunci-

ated very clearly in the most friendly old aunt kind of way, "Don't worry, dear, I don't know what the hell I'm doing here, either, so we might as well pretend we belong here and have as much fun as we possibly can. Life is short. Ripeness is all." And that was it. No small talk, no introduction, nothing further, just that, and then immediately back to her rather reserved and formal "I am the Empress of something or other and I forgive you all," attitude. Her voice was as striking as her appearance, deep, rich, scratchy, surprisingly robust and earthy, despite what seemed to be a slightly affected upper class British accent, and vaguely familiar. But there was no time to think about it, and her kindness was just what I needed, I giggled and relaxed, and as the people running the workshop proved to be quite nice and not at all threatening, I was soon happy I'd come after all.

Each of us in turn had to introduce ourselves to the group—I managed to babble out something not too idiotic, and I learned from these introductions that my friend's name was Mildred, that she had had some experience in radio, and that she, as she put it, had always been a bit of a Shakespeare buff—she said this as if she had rehearsed it for hours, carefully emphasizing each word, and punching the last one hard, buffffff, like a little explosion, in her slightly snooty but rather engaging accent and her almost sultry voice, "My name is Mildred, I've had some experience in radio, and I've always been a bit of a Shakespeare buffffff," an announcement carved out as carefully as a Christmas turkey, rather as if she'd been saying, "There will always be an England," or, "All of Gaul is divided into three parts." There was something so utterly and absurdly incongruous about her presence in that pastel classroom with block walls and green chalkboards and little college desks, with everybody else dressed in shorts and tee shirts and assorted university summer wear—and her so much older and dressed as if she'd stepped directly out of Dickens, it was all so bizarre and interesting that my fascination with her kept me from feeling like some sort of imposter or freak—if Mildred could fit in there, then certainly I could.

Also, she had a funny look in her eye, in great contrast to the magnificent assurance of her dress and general lady of the manor demeanor—just there, in the eyes only, a kind of furtive, slightly desperate look, which was so puzzling and out of place with the rest of her that at first one thought one must have been mistaken about it, but one was not mistaken, it was there, a strange, haunted look about the eyes, staring out from a sea of perfume. It was a look I had seen before, and recently, but not the same place I'd heard the voice, and this was—this was—now you're going to think I'm quite insane when I tell you this, but it's the sort of association that, right or wrong, no matter how grotesque it seems, once the mind has made it, one can never quite separate the two images, the association is so powerful that—the look in Mildred's eyes reminded me, after I thought about it and searched for the image they were touching in my head—it reminded me of the look in the eyes of Martin Fisher Martin, the other most vivid person I met that summer.

Martin Fisher Martin was the name I had given him, because I'd decided he must be either a fisher or a marten, I didn't know which. Martin Fisher Martin was a small, furry, otter-like animal who lived in a forgotten little patch of ground behind some buildings in the middle of the campus, surrounded by trees, a small collection of cages full of redwing blackbirds, pigeons, shacks with small windows for falcons, and Martin's small, fenced-in compound. Martin Fisher Martin was about the size of a beagle, with dark fur and nice little claw-handy paws, too fat to be an otter, but something like, who paced back and forth, back and forth, in his little cage, and every once in a while climbed up a little ladder and slid morosely down a pathetic little sliding board into a small sad puddle at the bottom. Pad, pad, pad, went Martin Fisher Martin, hour after hour, day after day, and every evening I would take a walk after supper, mostly to get away from my husband, whose very presence would fill me with a kind of furious and hopeless boredom, and my walks always led me to poor caged desperate Martin, and we would stare at each other through the wire of his cage.

He had such deep, expressive, dark and tragic eyes, this little trapped furry thing, furtive, despondent, desperate, slightly insane, looking out at me, I can still see them clearly. And when I looked into Mildred's eyes, that's who I saw, the eyes of Martin Fisher Martin, it was the strangest thing, but the eyes were the same, they were the same. Martin was ill, if not physically, certainly mentally—you would be, too, if you were trapped in that little concentration camp of his, waiting for some horrible experiment to be performed upon you, examining with your paws the same leaves and same bits of garbage over and over, turning over the same faded candy bar wrapper, sliding down your idiotic slide, staring through the wire of your prison, then tearing yourself away again to prowl mechanically, rolling your weight from side to side, padding from one mole-claw foot to the other, feet of ancient mummified babies he had, Egyptian feet, as leathery as the face of my friend

Mildred the Shakespeare bufffff. I observed his torment every evening and I did nothing, and now when I think of that time in my life I think of those two, Mildred and Martin Fisher Martin, inextricably entwined in my memory, the same frantic look in their eyes.

Everybody in the class had to do a monologue or a two person scene in front of the others, and monologues frightened me, they were too much like my life, so I ended up with a young man I rather liked, doing the nunnery scene from *Hamlet*, and one evening I took my walk, as usual, but I didn't go past the cage of my friend Martin Fisher Martin, I went instead to the young actor's apartment, to rehearse our scene. The thing was, I didn't tell my husband that's where I was going. He thought I was just taking my usual walk. I knew I should have told him. But I didn't. And I knew why I didn't. There he was, devouring the *Columbus Dispatch* in his stocking feet, and I had no desire to tell him anything, ever. I went down a little alley behind a hamburger establishment on High Street, past fenced-in backyards and trash cans, to a little red converted coach house where the actor lived, up a flight of black iron stairs, to the gabled door on the second floor, and the young man let me in, and we rehearsed our scene in his living room, and one thing led to another, and soon Hamlet and Ophelia were improvising a rather fierce love scene, and then I was lying on my back on his carpet, looking up at the sloped ceiling while Hamlet was undressing me, slowly and lovingly, kissing each part of me tenderly as he uncovered it, so different from my husband, until I lay trembling under his hands, naked and shuddering, and then he pulled off his tee shirt and bluejeans and everything and entered gently into me, Hamlet doing it to Ophelia there on the floor, and the boards under the rug were creaking and the pull down light above me was swaying back and forth and I was holding onto him and sobbing. Art is wonderful.

When I got home, my husband was watching a baseball game on television. I took a shower and went to bed.

The next day we did our scene in front of the group, at least, the part Shakespeare wrote. Hamlet was supposed to be a fox, and Ophelia was a chicken, and the fox was snapping at and teasing the chicken, you see, preparatory to devouring her, and there was so much sexual tension left over from our rehearsal that it bled into the scene, and the scene was good. I was a good actress, if acting was deception and betrayal, it was easy, as easy as deceiving one's husband, and they applauded us, and I had this vision of them all sitting around in the actor's apartment, watching us do it on the floor and cheering us on. And then an emaciated and nervous young Jewish man did Shylock's speech, Hath not a Jew eyes? if you prick us, do we not bleed? — that one, and although he was not really a very skilled actor, it clearly meant a great deal to him, and that bled into the scene, too, and although too much bleeding of real emotion into art does not always make for a pleasing outcome, it gave his performance a kind of genuine dignity that went beyond his skills as an actor, and I was pleased, and instructed, and happy for him, and strangely troubled, and then it was my friend Mildred's turn.

Mildred had chosen a monologue, one that seemed to be just as important to her as the Shylock one had been to the pale young man, only for reasons which I did not then understand, but still, even not understanding, it was strangely electric, what she did, in its own odd way. It was Lady Macbeth, lines pasted together from the sleepwalking scene, and her acting was quite melodramatic, as grotesque sense of pride or guilt combining to give us this cryptic hint about her true identity. Then I found her picture, black and white, making her way through customs, and I recognized without a doubt the person who, thirty years later, was to become my Shakespearean compatriot, Mildred of the white hair and lace blouses, Mildred the perfume-drenched Shakespeare bufffff, with the eyes of Martin Fisher Martin looking out at me.

And it was then, looking at this old picture, that I remembered other eyes, looking out of other pictures, eyes I hadn't thought about in years, the eyes of a large family of people I had seen pictures of in the house of my best friend in high school, a girl whose exotic mother was of Romanian gypsy blood. The pictures, preserved in an old family album, were of my friend's mother's family. They were taken in Europe in the thirties, and were of beautiful dark eyed people, old men, young boys, women and young girls and little children and old women, all of whom had been murdered by doctors conducting certain hideous medical experiments at Dachau, or perished in the gas chambers shortly thereafter.

I never saw Mildred again, nor did I keep in touch with the young actor who played Hamlet, but I did continue to visit Martin Fisher Martin until one evening in the fall I found him inexplicably gone, his cage torn down. I stood there looking at the empty space and discovered I was crying. I had just about worked up the courage to leave my husband when I found out I was pregnant, and so I stayed, and the following spring, nine months after my rehearsal of the nunnery scene, my daughter was born. She looks more like the actor every day. She's nine years old now, and I'm still with my husband. Perhaps I'll leave him soon, I don't know, I don't want to risk losing my little girl. That's the worst thing about betrayal, that it ties you so hideously to who or what you've betrayed. I see the actor sometimes on television, on a soap opera. He's not really a very good actor; I was much better. I keep thinking about Mildred, and the monologue she did. I can still see her there, sweating in front of that green chalkboard, holding her scented white handkerchief and croaking out her soul to us: "Out damned spot, out I say. One, two, why, then, 'tis time to do't. Hell is murky . . . here's the smell of blood still: all the perfumes of Arabia will not sweeten this little hand . . ." I remember the frantic look in her eyes when she said this, and then I remember the eyes of the children in my friend's pictures, and I do not feel pity for her. And sometimes after I've taken a shower I look in the mirror at my naked body, which is still quite nice, and I think of the actor making love to me, and I caress myself, perform the act again in my imagination for the audience of one reflected image in the mirror, and then I look in my eyes, and see looking back at me the eyes of poor Martin Fisher Martin, desperate and frantic in his cage, waiting in despair for his inevitable end.

(*The light fades on her and goes out.*)

How Many Children Had Lady MacBeth?

How Many Children Had
Lady MacBeth?

*(There is one character, BONNIE, a pretty young woman
of thirty, barefoot, wearing a leotard and bluejeans,
on a bare stage with just one high stool. As she begins
to speak to us, she will take off the bluejeans and
begin to do gentle actor's stretches and warmups
while she talks, using the floor and the stool. As she
gets more involved in her story, she will warm up less,
and by the last part she will be sitting on the stool, just
talking to us.)*

BONNIE. Actors have always known the Scottish play
is haunted, and some of them have very definite rules
about it — you must never quote it backstage, and if you
must refer to it, you never say its title, you call it the
Scottish play, or sometimes even *a certain* Scottish play.
And this curse that's on it is supposed to account for the
great number of perfectly dreadful productions of it, although in fact most productions of most plays are pretty
dreadful, when you come right down to it, especially of
Shakespeare. There is, you see, an unspoken mythology
perpetrated by crummy directors and producers who
think people are stupid so plays should also be stupid,
that the easier a play is to put on adequately, the better
the play is, which, if it were true, would make *Barefoot in
the Park* a much better play than *King Lear*. I think it's
this cretinous myth that's led modern playwrights to
allow directors and producers to coax, harass, cajole,
threaten and intimidate them into hacking away whatever is most brave and subtle and complex and different
and interesting in their work, leaving finally only a kind

91

of oatmeal the director feels less threatened by — the rule seems to be, if we can't make it work in the first rehearsal, it's the play's fault, cut it, when of course anybody who's worked on Shakespeare or Chekhov or for that matter anything of value knows that it's usually those things that worked so well in the first rehearsal that have grown so stale and dead by the week before opening that they have to be redone anyway, while those very parts of the play that seemed most impossible early on, that you had to bang your head against again and again, screaming and swearing and crying and getting you horribly frustrated until in a fit of despair or out of utter exhaustion an entirely different reading from somewhere suddenly flows out of you, and it's not at all what you expected but it works and turns out to be the best moment in the production. But with new plays this seldom gets a chance to happen, because the best parts get cut in rehearsal, and that's part of the reason most contemporary drama really sucks, that and greed and a lot of other things I don't want to talk about right now because I don't want to get too angry, I've got to go be Mariana in the moated grange this evening — *Measure for Measure*, one of Willy's secret best. Not such a great part, though, but I don't care, I'll do Shakespeare any time, any where, to my agent's increasing fury and at the expense of a great many long-running national dog food and deodorant commercials I might have lived quite comfortably on. I've done four Mirandas, three Cordelias, I just did Ophelia in New Jersey, but my favorite play, for some reason, has always been the Scottish play, and the role I always wanted was Lady Mac.

I'd been in other productions of it, playing various kinds of female set decoration, an attending gentle-woman, a very young and more or less naked witch, and

I must confess to you, all of these productions were major or minor disasters of one sort or another. People got whacked or mauled in the fight scenes, lights fell near people's heads, there were two bomb threats, one of which, the one where I was the naked young witch, I'm convinced was called in by Shakespeare himself. My favorite bad production of my favorite play was the one in which a certain attendant Lord was to carry on the dead body of Lady Mac just as the words were spoken, The Queen, my Lord, is dead. Well, this particular Lady Mac was an ex-movie star who'd put on quite a bit of weight — Lady Big Mac, we called her — they always come back to their roots in the theatre when they get too fat for the camera — and the big strong fellow whose job was to carry her dead body onstage had stepped off a platform in the dark and broken his ankle shortly before his entrance, and the only other actor available on the spur of the moment was a rather little fellow, but very macho, who insisted he could do it, no problem. So he hoisted the Amazon Lady M into his arms and staggered onstage just as the cue line, The Queen, my Lord, is dead, was spoken, lost his balance, and fell over backwards with the poor dead Queen on top of him. Well, the audience lost it, and then Macbeth lost it, and ended up giggling his way through his Tomorrow and tomorrow speech, and, well, on the whole, high tragedy it was not.

I was in another production in which one of the witches fainted from the heat in the middle of her scene and fell head first into the cauldron, and another in which a drunk in the alley behind the theatre kept playing a terrible version of *Tea for Two* on an accordion as loudly as possible during the sleepwalking scene. This was the same production where poor MacDuff developed a mental block about a rather familiar Shakespear-

ean phrase, and every night, when learning of the murder
of his wife and children burst out with

What, all my pretty chickens and their dam, in one
swell foop?

But despite all this, I continued to love the play, and
still longed desperately to play Lady Mac, although for a
long time my ingenue looks kept me from even being
considered for it. Finally, I got the chance. I was under-
studying a much older woman, who obligingly ran into a
door backstage just before curtain and broke her nose—
I was nowhere near her at the time, I swear—and so I
had to go on in her place. It seemed like fate. I knew I was
going to be terrific. I felt that I understood this character,
everything about her, her ambition—I'm an actress,
God knows I understand that—her frustration—same
there—her impatience with her husband—I was married to a nice man who wanted me to quit acting and stay
home and have babies, and when he finally realized I was
never going to stop and take time for that, he was gone. I
had dared things, I had fought, I had sacrificed, I had
endured, and now, finally, I was getting my chance to
play her. It was destiny. And it went very well, I mean,
extremely well—I'd been waiting all my life to play this
role, and the audience, which had at first been disap-
pointed it was me, began to realize they were seeing
something special, and their resentment began to turn
into appreciation, they were with the play, they were lost
in it, I could feel them rooting for me, they were with me,
it was the best performance of our run, the old respected
dull hag of a Lady M had been transformed unexpectedly into a hot and sexy younger version, that is, me, and
I played the sensuality for all it was worth, and an odd
kind of innocence, and humor, my Lady M had a sense
of humor, and pathos, but she was hard as nails, but she

had this tenderness, it was working, everything was working, the magic was there, the gods were present, old Will was beaming at us, Macbeth was actually paying attention to his wife for once, it was flowing, it was stunning, and then came the sleepwalking scene, oh, it was going so well, it was going so well, until the moron playing the Doctor, who had had a couple of drinks before the show, and seemed hypnotized by my boobs, tripped and knocked the candle over and set my nightgown on fire.

I decided to try and play it, use it, pretend we had planned it that way, it was part of the madness, see, and the girl playing the gentlewoman was quick enough to grab the bucket we had onstage, in which I was trying to wash the bloodstains off my hands, and throw it on me. The bloodstains were imaginary, but, fortunately the water was not, the bucket was nearly full, for some reason, and I was soaked, but, dammit, this was my moment, I wasn't going to let it slip away for anything, and the audience was so into it, I think they would have bought it, considered it a bit of daring technical tour de force on the director's part — I looked like the winner of a wet nightgown contest, and that alone might have kept them watching and wanting to believe, if only the gung ho assistant stage manger, who had the hots for me and was about three times too hyper for his job anyway, had not then run out onto the stage, yelled for everybody not to panic, and fire extinguished me.

I don't know. Maybe we should have gone with *Barefoot in the Park*. I built my whole life towards a moment when I was set on fire, drenched and then covered in foam in front of six hundred people. Sometimes acting is like being punished for a crime you didn't commit. Oh, well. I'll get another chance, some day. They usually cast her much too old, so I'll get a turn or two in middle age.

The problem is, I've been having this odd fantasy lately. I see my children watching me play Lady Macbeth. I want my children to see me do it. Isn't that crazy? I don't have any children. And as the years go by, it becomes increasingly unlikely that I ever will, and I miss them. I miss my children. I feel like I ran off with Shakespeare and abandoned them. You make choices and then there are consequences, and then the consequences have consequences, and for a long time you don't notice this happening, because you're young and busy and have things to do and things you want and no time to stop and think about it, but the consequences just keep happening, every moment of your life has a consequence, somewhere down the line. She didn't really understand that when she made him kill the king. But consequences don't care if you understand them or not, they just keep happening, tomorrow and tomorrow, to the last syllable of recorded time. Shakespeare knew. That son of a bitch knew everything. He had children.

Poor babies. I wrote them out of my play. All my pretty ones. In one swell foop. I guess it's a curse.

(*The light fades on her and goes out.*)

Notes from the
Moated Grange

Notes from the Moated Grange

(There is one character, MARIANA, who stands, beautiful and weary, by the light shining through an autumn stained glass window — the light is visible, the window is not — looking much as she does in the painting by John Everett Millais.)

MARIANA. Most of love is waiting. I am a secret person. I wait. I am a waitress. I am the secret agent of his forgotten lust. I wait for him. I am the one who waits. Here in the moated grange, my waiting room. There are bats at night, they wheel and squeak and flutter about. I watch the birds, I grow to know them well, I see the little goldfinch pecking maniacally at her reflection in the glass. Like me. I look in the mirror. I am frightened by my beauty. No one sees it. It will die and no one will know. There is no one to paint me.

There are fish in the moat. One big one always waits for me at the little wooden bridge. He looks up at me. My love is a cold fish. I am his mistress. Promised and then lost. He will perhaps soon send to have me killed. He lusts for another, a nun, I believe. I meditate upon the bed trick. It always seems to work. She will come soon and propose it to me, and I will no doubt accept. And yet — And yet a part of me wants this loneliness. It is something nobody can understand. There is something about loneliness that is strangely intoxicating, enchanted, I don't know how else to explain it, talking to yourself, living in your head, creating universes in your mind like a forgotten playwright. Being alone is like being God, you must make the world in your head.

My brother was lost at sea. I look in the water and think of him. At the bottom of the ocean it must be very peaceful. His eyes, looking up. I, too, am surrounded completely by water, I am the very definition of an island. The moat defines me. In the murk at the bottom of the moat are skeletons of countless dead men. You can see the bubbles come up when they break wind.

Good works go with my name. When my brother miscarried at sea, in that perished vessel was my dowry. This was the wreckage of my love, for with no dowry, Angelo the Righteous did abandon me. The Bible book I am is Lamentations.

Love is illness. I love one who is not worthy to kiss my toes. His cruelty only entraps me more, fills me with anger, and a kind of violent longing. I miss him desperately. Why is this the case? Men love cruel women, women love cruel men. I take no pleasure in my suffering, yet I cause myself to suffer. I must be strong. I have a mind and I must use it. If he is cruel to me, then I must be cruel to him, measure for measure. And yet, and yet — this rule is very hard. The bed trick, the bed trick, oh, love is merely a madness. Who said that? Some jackass.

I do not like this Isabella person, she is cold, cold, she would let them dangle Claudio her brother from the gallows for the sake of her virginity. Virginity. It's like suspended animation. And personally, I like having a dead brother, it makes him so much closer, somehow. Like a dead playwright, he can no longer annoy me by changing his lines. And then she comes to me, with this horrible monk who is not a monk, who is in reality the vile unkind attractive old fantastical duke of dark corners, I recognize him, I know him, he lives in the dark and eats my brain, he will return to execute my love, he is the cannibal god, he will marry this nun, no bride of Christ she, and they will make the beast together on the winter bed of their hypocrisy.

Now listen, listen, I'm going to tell you a true thing, the truest thing I know, and that is simply this—that in God's world, anyone can have anything they want, absolutely anything, whate'er their hearts desire, on one condition—that condition being they can only have it once they no longer want it. Once you cease to desire the beloved, who has scorned you cruelly, humiliated you, turned from you, left you a fool among snickering idiots, once you finally, painfully, after years of suffering, have taught yourself indifference—then, then, then the beloved comes to you with open arms, having been rejected by their own cruel lover, sees now your true worth, is relieved to settle for you, be safe in your love, enjoy taking you for granted happily ever after. This is the geography of love's prison. This is the secret of the moated grange. Eliminate desire, the master said, and you can have anything you no longer want. This is the ultimate truth of the universe.

So, why, having painfully deciphered this from the cryptogram of my experience, am I not happy, am I not resigned to my fate, at peace with myself? Well, I am, or would be, except, except, except, in the night, in the dark of the night, under a red moon, bleeding, he comes to me, his phantom comes to me, the phantom of the one I have tried to teach myself not to love, and he does cruel things to me that make me shudder and cry out.

Here in the moated grange, no matter what you fancy, the stillness and the complex choreography of birds cannot heal you, for you are made of deceit and have a wound that cannot heal except by death. You have been formed, a kind of accident, a minor character in a dark play, you are merely functional, and then, the performance being over, you are buried in a trunk and left backstage.

Here in the moated grange we play the bed trick. Here in the moated grange we love the unworthy. Here in the moated grange we forever wait. And when at last our beloved comes to us, chastised, forgiven, ready to be our humble servant forever, we look warmly upon him and embrace him gratefully, sobbing, and then, when he turns his back to contemplate the moon, we press our foot firmly against his rump and propel him head first into the moat.

Did I tell you it was stocked with carniverous fish? I wonder if he can swim?

(*The lights go out.*)

Full Fathom Five

Full Fathom Five

*(There is one character, MIRANDA, a young girl, on a
bare stage which is the shore of her island, looking
out over the water, speaking to the audience.)*

MIRANDA. Do you ever get the feeling somebody's
watching you? I do. I ask my father about it and he just
smiles at me. My father makes things, he's a kind of
wizard, he creates, he's the god of this island, and I am
one of his creations. He has a box of analogies he fashions
into animals and people. I am part of his dreams. He's a
playwright. He fashions universes like the God of Gen-
esis. This is his magic garden. We play out his fantasies
on the stage of this island. A piece of theatre is like the
collective dream of the audience, my father says a madman told him once. A gaggle of people get together in a
particular place at a particular time and focus on a stage,
and on that stage a dream happens, and they share it. It's
like you drew a circle, as in summoning up demons in
nigromancy, and agreed that, within the circle, the
dream would live. Break the circle and it vanishes. The
chief dreamer, who furnishes the dream for the others,
my father, is the playwright god who makes a little world
and watches it run. Tick tock. Like a lovely maniacal
clockworks. I was born into this universe as its heroine.
And thereby hangs a tale. This is it, Adam, that grieves
me.

My father tells me I should stop bathing in melancholy
and enjoy the beauty of the role I play, and I would prefer
to believe that he is right. This world, he says, is quite
literally a stage; before we entered it, in that other place
called death, that is, offstage, we chose the part we wished
to play here, and it was one of the rules of death that if we

were to play in this play, we had to agree to forget completely who we were in the other place, offstage, and live the role we'd chosen, here, on this great stage of fools, until its proper end, whatever that may be. Then, the play being over, we go back down the tunnel to the other place, death, backstage, our dressing room, where we remember once again our other selves, our non-performing selves, ourselves in death, outside the play, backstage, and think about our performance, and choose our next role. If the world is thus, then all suffering is freely chosen by the sufferer, in the same way an actor might choose a role in a play, King Lear, say. The actor, choosing to play King Lear, knows full well that his character must suffer enormously in the playing out of his inevitable action. But he chooses it, for the experience, it is a freely chosen role, so there is no cruelty in the creator, you see, he merely writes the play and then allows us to cast ourselves in it if we choose. My father even suggested that the place at the end of the tunnel, the backstage area, was in fact also itself another stage, that in another country down another tunnel one had chosen to be an actor who played the role of an actor who played the role of Lear, or me, or whoever, so on and so on, in an infinite series of theatrical Chinese boxes in boxes. He said the world in which he created me and our island had in turn been created by a man named Shakespeare, who wrote many universes besides my favorite one about Lear, which I had stupidly been under the impression my father wrote, but who himself was a character in a play by some Italian playwright, who was in turn a character in a play by someone named Jehovah, who was in turn a character in a play by somebody named Moses, who was in turn a character in a play by some other creator god named I think Cecil B. DeMille, etcetera, to the last syllable of recorded backwards forewards and sideways time. We live, said my father, at the bottom of an infinite ocean of plays within plays.

It occurred to me after observing what a liar Caliban could be, that perhaps my father was also lying, that all of this could be merely another one of his experimental fantasies, so I confronted him with my suspicions, and he replied that of course he was a liar, of course this play within play within play theory of the universe was entirely his fantasy, but that it was a very nice and useful fantasy, in that it corresponded in every respect to what appeared to be the reality of the play that was our daily life, it was an explanation that worked, and therefore it was very good magic, and a great deal more sensible than most religion.

I think it was then that I decided my father was dangerously insane, and that it was probably my duty to kill him. It was the accumulated suffering, you see, the suffering of the animals, the inevitable, unspeakably multiplied murder upon murder of which his universe was made, all over the island, things eating things and then being eaten by other things, it was so horrible, beautiful when you don't look too closely, but then unmistakeably hideous.

It seemed to me that the most evil thing in the universe must be creation itself, because creation is what makes suffering. If there were not creation, then there would be no suffering. I thought I had it all figured out, and although I love my father too much to actually kill him, I did my best to annoy him as much as I could by hiding his spectacles and spending a lot of time in the bathroom. I thought the more I could distract him, the less he would have time to create, and the less he created the less suffering there would be, but then, unfortunately, I was attacked by the most insidious calamity of all — the monstrosity called sex. I was going to say love, but the distinction is in my mind a great deal blurrier than most of the time I have the courage to admit.

Of Caliban's repeated attempts to ravish me as I sunbathed on the beach, the less said the better. My father loves losing his temper, is especially fond of playing scenes of righteous indignation, but the fact is, that pathetic little troglodyte couldn't ravish an inflatable woman. As for Ferdinand, well, he proved to be accomplished enough at heavy petting to get me worked up to a frenzy, at which point his justifiable terror of my father's wrath would cause him to remove his finger and take three laps around the island. But I got the general idea, enough to convince me that this tragic comedy of love and sex is the summit of the satanic creator's evil, in that, in order to prevent us from acting on our realization that all creation leads to destruction and unhappiness, along comes puberty, and one finds oneself desperate to engage in ridiculous and degrading acts designed by the same insidious god to lead, inevitably, to the creation of a whole new little actor on the cosmic stage, a screaming, bloody, shitting and pissing, mucus-filled character actor, a conglomeration of grief and horror so profoundly and obnoxiously compelling as to be beyond belief, that essence of entrapment and deceit, death's trump card, a helpless newborn thing.

I asked my father about this, hoping to get some sound advice on birth control, but my father was not helpful. You were just such a creature, he said. Your mother and I created you. And lived to regret it, I said. That's not true, said my father. Your mother died. Anyway, you see, he said, it does one absolutely no good to regret one's creations, just because one can see very clearly that one is

going to come, despite all good sense, to be desperately
and insanely attached to them, that they are going to give
one endless hours of worry and agony, that they will take
us for granted and be horribly misused by others. If poor
Willy Shakespeare, he said, the author of the universe in
which I authored you, could see how abysmally his universes are enacted in other universes I have observed
with my interdimensional spyglass, the botched lines,
the grotesque overacting, the simpering, whimpering,
smirking, leering, stuffy, smartassedly affected trendy or
moth-eaten crap they make routinely of his carefully
crafted universes, he might wish for a moment that he
had never given them birth, but that is neither here nor
there, for the fact is, he chose to, and he had no choice but
to choose to, and he chose to anyway, he is responsible,
and there are consequences of his making and he is responsible, beyond his making though they may have
been, nevertheless, there it is, one makes what one
makes, one copulates because one copulates, universe
within universe, intercourse being the penetration of one
universe into another, ejaculating matter inward that
will merge with other matter and grow into another universe, forever and ever, to the last syllable of recorded
time.

Is that in this play? I asked him.

I don't remember, he said. And it doesn't matter. A
million monkeys at a million typewriters wrote this play.
Shakespeare wrote this play. I wrote this play. You write
this play, each breath you take is a moment of stage time,
each word you say is recorded on some demented Italian
man's typewriter. I pretend to hate this young man of
yours, this Ferdinand, he says. I do hate him. For one
thing, I hate his name. It sounds like a bull. But it doesn't
matter if I hate him or not. You are, irrespective of my

wishes, sooner or later going to allow him to invade your womb with battalions of sperm no matter what I say or do. This is the insidious nature of creation. This is the nature of the great theatre of the world. It is a tragedy. It is a comedy. It is beyond all the cretinous categories ever devised by the ditsy little minds of all the flatulent crapulous critics and theorists in the history of history. It is all of the above. It is none of the above. It is play within play within play, world without end. Ripeness is all.

Did you write that? I asked.

I don't think so, says my father, kisses my head absently, and wanders off down the beach to his favorite crawdad pool.

I sit and brood and look at the ocean. Out across the water, another storm is brewing, to take us home, perhaps, or to bury us beneath the waters. I don't know. Perhaps I will take off all my clothes and swim in the ocean. Possibly there will be sharks. Perhaps Ferdinand will jump in and rescue me, drag me to shore, and, overwhelmed by the beauty of my nubile, budding, ripening young body, he will make passionate, desperate love to me on the sand. Perhaps the spirits of the island will watch us. It sounds like a play. Or perhaps I'll just go torment Caliban. He's tied to a tree now. He goes berserk when I show him one of my breasts. Once when I was doing this, I had the strongest most unmistakeable impression yet that somebody was watching me, not one of the island spirits, but someone else, some foreigner, out in the darkness. I looked out at the ocean, and there was nothing. But I had the strangest feeling there were people out there in the dark, looking at me. And one young man especially, imaginary, no doubt, transfigured by the unexpected vision of my erect nipple, our eyes met for a moment, me in the light, him in the darkness, and then everything went black, and there was the sound of clapping everywhere, and he went away from me, down a dark tunnel, to write a play, perhaps. Those who wait in darkness, the lost ones, those who are beyond redemption, waiting to be redeemed. Buried beneath the waters of time, the drowned ones. In the audience of death. I see his eyes still in the darkness, beneath the waters, like pearls. This is my island. And I'm going to wait here for him. And I will never leave it. Never.

(*The light fades on her and goes out.*)

Other Publications for Your Interest

THE CURATE SHAKESPEARE AS YOU LIKE IT
(LITTLE THEATRE—COMEDY)

By DON NIGRO

4 men, 3 women—Bare stage

This extremely unusual and original piece is subtitled: "The record of one company's attempt to perform the play by William Shakespeare". When the very prolific Mr. Nigro was asked by a professional theatre company to adapt *As You Like It* so that it could be performed by a company of seven he, of course, came up with a completely original play about a rag-tag group of players comprised of only seven actors led by a dotty old curate who nonetheless must present Shakespeare's play; and the dramatic interest, as well as the comedy, is in their hilarious attempts to impersonate all of Shakespeare's multitude of characters. The play has had numerous productions nationwide, all of which have come about through word of mouth. We are very pleased to make this "underground comic classic" widely available to theatre groups who like their comedy wide open and theatrical.   (#5742)

SEASCAPE WITH SHARKS AND DANCER
(LITTLE THEATRE—DRAMA)

By DON NIGRO

1 man, 1 woman—Interior

This is a fine new play by an author of great talent and promise. We are very glad to be introducing Mr. Nigro's work to a wide audience with *Seascape With Sharks and Dancer*, which comes directly from a sold-out, critically acclaimed production at the world-famous Oregon Shakespeare Festival. The play is set in a beach bungalow. The young man who lives there has pulled a lost young woman from the ocean. Soon, she finds herself trapped in his life and torn between her need to come to rest somewhere and her certainty that all human relationships turn eventually into nightmares. The struggle between his tolerant and gently ironic approach to life and her strategy of suspicion and attack becomes a kind of war about love and creation which neither can afford to lose. In other words, this is quite an offbeat, wonderful love story. We would like to point out that the play also contains a wealth of excellent **monologue** and **scene material.**   (#21060)